D1280797

Camino Sunrise

Walking With My Shadows

One reluctant pilgrim
packs a weighty load
on a 500-mile path

Reginald Spittle

Cover and illustrations by Sue Spittle

Camino Sunrise
Reginald Spittle

The events in this book are real and conversations have been recreated from the author's memory. Some names have been changed. Details about places, such as accommodations, are based on the author's memory and notes. Prices and distances are approximate.
This is an account of my Camino trek and is not meant to be used as a guide.

spittlereg@gmail.com
Published by Reginald Spittle
Ashland, Oregon

ISBN 13: (e-book) 978-1-7328909-0-9
ISBN 13: (paperback) 978-1-7328909-1-6

For Andrew, Brad and Chris

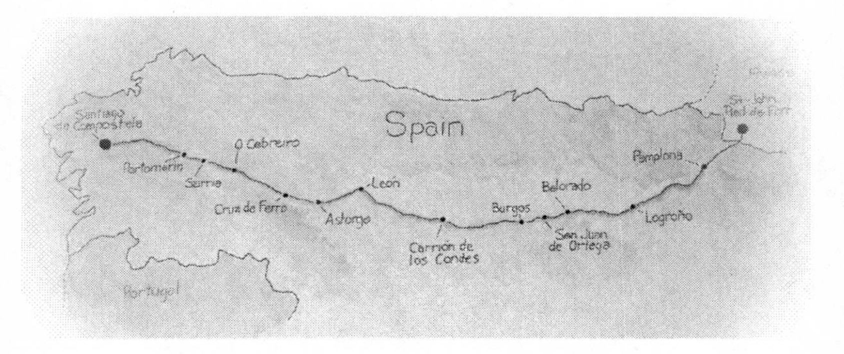
Spain
Santiago de Compostela
Portomarin
Sarria
O Cebreiro
Cruz de Ferro
Astorga
León
Carrión de los Condes
Burgos
Belorado
San Juan de Ortega
Logroño
Pamplona
Portugal

1

We Can't Do That!

On a warm August night, I loaded dinner plates into the dishwasher at our California home near Yosemite National Park. I tossed a question to my wife Sue, who was settling onto a couch in our living room.

"How about a movie?"

"If you think you can stay awake."

Sue liked to poke fun at my television viewing habits, but so what if I slept through three episodes of House Hunters the night before? The show worked better than sleeping pills for me.

I peeled open the red-and-white Netflix envelope and inserted the disc, as I had done countless times. We settled in for movie night with cups of hot chamomile tea.

"That was a great movie," I said. "I was awake the whole time!"

She concentrated on the movie credits.

"Did you like it?" I asked.

I could depend on an honest opinion. Sue squinted, a sign she was measuring her response.

"We should do it."

The words arrived like an ambush.

"Do what? Walk 500 miles? We can't do that!"

I waited for her to laugh and say, "I was only kidding!"

Instead, she leaned toward me. "But what if we can?"

The movie was *The Way*, starring Martin Sheen as Tom, a career-oriented American ophthalmologist. His son, Daniel (played by real-life son Emilio Estevez), sets off to walk 500 miles on the Camino de Santiago, a pilgrimage across northern Spain that has drawn millions for hundreds of years. Daniel dies during a snow-storm in the Pyrenees Mountains on his first day, bringing his dad from California to St. Jean Pied de Port, France to collect his son's ashes. St. Jean is the traditional beginning of the trek that ends in Santiago.

The day after arriving in France, Tom impulsively sets out to do what his rebellious only child had implored him to do just before leaving for Spain: "Walk with me, Dad." He carries his son's full backpack that also holds Daniel's ashes. Tom's heart leaves little room for other pilgrims, but as he sprinkles Daniel's ashes along the Camino, his mood lightens while he forges life-changing relationships with three trekkers.

Five hundred miles and many lessons later, Tom ultimately understands his son's words: "You don't choose a life, Dad, you live one."

It was a compelling and moving story, but as I processed Sue's suggestion, I felt knots in my stomach. Tom slept in communal bunk rooms with strangers. Would there be shared shower rooms? I was so self-conscious that I avoided changing my clothes in front of camping buddies. Also, I would have to carry a backpack and keep up with people half (or a third) my age who might poke fun at me. Finally, I loved hiking, but 500 miles? No way!

I looked at Sue, who awaited my reply. My right hand gripped my thigh as I blurted out an emotional response.

"But I don't know if I can handle the dorms and bathrooms. And I hate backpacking."

Sue knew I was on the defensive. "What else are we going to do with our time now that we're retired?"

I searched for a way out.

"I'm tired. I'm going to bed."

Sue contained her frustration, but I knew I was just delaying further discussion. During the movie, it never occurred to me that we could (or would) do the Camino.

I was wrong to think that my bed would ease my tension. As I sought sleep, my mind sent me once again to a dark corner of its video library. It was physical education class on my first day of seventh grade, an event I had ruminated about since the last day of sixth grade. I stood in front of my locker and stacked the new white t-shirt, blue shorts, and jock strap on a wooden bench. My heartbeat accelerated as I pulled off my Goodwill t-shirt, my too-short trousers, and, so grudgingly, my tattered JC Penney briefs.

"Hey, look at Spittle," shouted Eddie, whose manly voice taunted me in sixth grade. "I've seen more meat on a chicken." He leaped at me and snapped his towel at my butt. It stung sharply and when I reopened my eyes, I saw 30-some boys, in various stages of undress, sneering at me. Their laughter hurt worse than the towel's strike. Nearly a half century later, I still bled from the wounds.

That junior high was one of five schools I attended in sixth and seventh grades as my father moved our family from one rundown trailer park to another. I attended 13 schools as a child and my name, "Reginald Spittle," usually brought snickers and whispers when a teacher introduced me to a class. It was often worse on the playground, where I was peppered with insults about my out-of-style second-hand clothes, bird-like legs, and bowl haircut.

All my life, I obsessed over the most trivial embarrassments. As a kid, PE activities, especially games that required catching a ball, were like torture chambers. Team captains always chose me last and if a ball came my way, I wanted to run away and hide. I would have easily won the "least athletic" yearbook award.

As an adult, I was still intimidated by new situations where one misstep became a shadow that haunted me for days, weeks, even longer. I sought protection like a turtle, recoiling when I felt someone might find my vulnerabilities. I was a slave to anxiety and hid behind a veneer that looked like confidence to those who thought they knew me.

The Way may have been a good movie, but as I lay in bed battling my spiraling imagination, I wished I had never ordered it. I feared that life on the Camino would leave me without a hiding place.

I heard the toilet flush and knew Sue was coming to bed.

I rolled onto my side. "Grow up, Reg," I thought. "The Camino is not junior high."

When Sue crawled into bed, I pretended to be asleep, but a question loomed.

When will I finally learn to trust myself—and those around me—so I can let go of the past and feel peace?

2

One Slip and I'm Dead

During the rest of August and into November, my mind was like a yo-yo when I mulled over the Camino. At its apex, I felt the magic of one of the world's most famous pilgrimages and the sense of accomplishment I would feel as I walked into Santiago after 500 miles. At its low point, I was in a communal dorm room or bathroom, too embarrassed to show my skimpy body, thinking everyone was watching me. Or, I was on the trail, struggling to carry my pack as younger, more athletic trekkers left me in their dust.

I feared the Camino would be like a school softball game, and I would be in right field, knees shaking, praying with all my might that no one would hit a ball to me.

My worries about backpacking dated back two decades. In 1992, I surprised myself and agreed to a backpacking trip to the top of Half Dome and Cloud's Rest in Yosemite National Park with friends Mike and Doug, who both carried confidence everywhere.

Usually, one or two kids at each of my schools saw through my out-of-style clothes and past my nerdiness to befriend a painfully insecure boy. They were my security blankets. Mike and Doug reminded me of those kids. Doug had become a close friend in only two years since Sue, the boys and I had moved to Mariposa County. When our families got together, we laughed, shared stories, and watched our children play. I was in awe of Doug's many talents; he was a star tennis player in college and had built three large, two-story houses since moving to Mariposa. Mike's friendship developed later and we shared days skiing and golfing, as well as taking our kids, who were enthusiastic sports fans, to pro and college baseball games. I golfed and skied in Mike's shadow, but he always made me feel like an equal. It had taken many years for me to reach this point, but my relationships with Doug and Mike built my self-confidence.

As I drove to the Yosemite commuter bus stop in Midpines the July morning of the backpacking trip, I was psyched about climbing Half Dome. I hoped I could remember to trust that Doug and Mike might laugh with me, but never at me, if my fear of heights and lack of backpacking skills showed. I longed to banish the ghosts from the past.

Mike and Doug waited in the gravel parking lot as I pulled in. I lifted my mother-in-law's aging exterior-frame backpack from the trunk of my car, expecting snickers or at least a comment. None came, but my brain quickly found the well-worn path to classmates' laughter when I showed up at school in thrift-store clothes. A new backpack was not in my family budget, and Mike and Doug understood that.

When the bus arrived, we took seats toward the back.

"Hey, Reg, I left room for the pasta." Mike opened the top of his modern, interior frame pack. I handed him the extra-large Ziploc bag crammed with spaghetti noodles I had cooked the night before to save us time at the high-altitude campsite that night. He nearly dropped it on the floor of the bus.

"Whoa! Is that frozen?" He and Doug burst into laughter at the prospect of having to carry enough frozen noodles to feed a troop of hungry guys. I had figured the pasta would thaw during our daylong trek, but failed to realize it would be as heavy as a block of ice. Mike and Doug are two of the most considerate guys I've ever known, but as I sat across from them, my inner voice raced back to my school-playground response. My throat tightened, my jaw clenched, my heartbeat quickened. My ghost allowed me only a nervous laugh as the bus rolled toward Yosemite Valley. Humiliation, instead of a sense of humor, was my seat mate.

After the bus climbed into Yosemite Valley, I caught glimpses of Half Dome in the morning sun and pictured myself standing at the top of the massive granite mountain that afternoon. It would be the greatest physical accomplishment of my life. The bus delivered us at our starting point for the Mist Trail and a steep trek of about eight miles to the wire cables leading to the top of Half Dome. I awkwardly put on my backpack and tried to look like I knew how to adjust the straps. My pack weighed about 40 pounds and felt heavier as I labored up the steep trail and rock stairs next to Vernal and Nevada falls.

Like a new backpack, a pair of hiking shoes was not in my budget, so I wore running shoes. It was a big mistake. I fell hard once, sliding down a rock slope and skinning my left leg and side. I also skidded and nearly fell many times on the granite, which the guys nicknamed "Reg rock" in an effort to lighten the mood.

As we walked, I was disappointed that I had once again taken myself too seriously. It must have been my brain that was frozen when I put the pasta in the freezer. My brain had not even thawed the next morning when I pulled out the huge ball of noodles to take to the bus for Mike's pack. How could I have not noticed the weight? It would have made a great Laurel and Hardy skit. It was a stupid mistake, and my reaction made it worse.

I vowed to nurture my sense humor on this trip, but I knew my nature would resist.

We climbed 4,000 feet on stairs and switchbacks, around the back of Half Dome, to the cables on the curved side near its flat face. The slope to the top is so steep that climbers pull themselves up using metal cables attached to poles imbedded in the granite slope.

As we arrived, two hikers looked up at the cables. I was glad they were not behind me because they would be speedier climbers, if age was a factor. The man pulled his gloves tight, then showed the woman how to begin the climb before he jumped back down. It was clear that it was not his first time on Half Dome.

"You go first; I'll be right behind you."

She grabbed one cable with her right hand and froze.

"I can't do it." She cried, turned around and walked away. He rushed to her side and guided her toward privacy.

I apprehensively eyed the wall that was the side of Half Dome. We had hidden our backpacks in bushes safely away from the trail. I squeezed my hands into gloves and faced the famous rock. I studied the parallel, thick wire cables, which were at waist height and were supported by metal poles. The poles were placed every four or five feet up the granite wall. Wooden slats anchored to the rock provided footholds.

"Slide one hand up the cable and grip the other side tightly," Doug directed. "Slip the other hand up. Keep one hand gripped on a cable." It sounded simple, but my arm strength paled compared to my hiking partners.

I grabbed the cables and pulled myself up to the first wooden slat. I inhaled deeply, then did something stupid. I looked down, to my right, and saw Yosemite Valley thousands of feet below. Instead of freezing and breaking into a sweat, I turned back toward the cables, then pulled myself up to the next slat. And the next.

"This is a piece of cake," I yelled back to Doug, perhaps too soon. Was I trying too hard to look calm?

Suddenly, two trekkers appeared ahead. They were coming down! There was only one set of cables. I froze, but before panic set in, the grizzled hikers above me each put both hands on the cable to my left and slowly descended toward me. I yanked my left hand to the righthand cable and clutched with both hands as if my life depended on it. I hoped they wouldn't notice my heebie-jeebies. After they passed, I gripped with my right hand as I seized the other cable with my left. I hauled myself up to the next board and, eventually, all the way to the top. For Doug and Mike, it was just one more time atop Half Dome.

I tried to be cool and contain my excitement, but I knew I had earned an "I Made It to the Top!" hat sold in the Yosemite gift shop. Maybe a matching t-shirt too.

My achievement took me back to the summer when I was 13 years old. I stood chest-deep in a swimming hole near Casitas Springs, California and watched other kids from my trailer park jump into a deep area from the rocky ledge high above.

"Come on, Spittle, try it!" they shouted several times, followed by laughter that I interpreted as ridicule. I was the only one who stayed below.

This time, 27 years later, I had left my demon at the base of the Half Dome cables.

I watched from a distance as Doug and Mike stood near the edge of Half Dome, looking at Yosemite Valley more than 4,000 feet below. I slowly turned around, taking in the spectacular 360-degree view of the snow-capped Sierra Nevada peaks. I snapped a few photographs with my disposable Kodak camera. Some of the 40 or so other trekkers crawled on their stomachs to peer over the edge at the canyon, which had been carved by a glacier thousands of years before. I remained far from the rim.

Standing atop the 8,839-foot dome, I turned to my right, toward our next goal: Cloud's Rest, a narrow peak that stood 9,931 feet tall. I was surprised that I felt little apprehension about my next day's challenge. I had no idea that my tenuous climbing confidence would face a rival unlike any I had ever encountered.

After a half hour atop Half Dome, we put on our gloves and reversed our steps down the cables. Thankfully, our packs were still where we left them. On the way down, I was prepared for a panic attack that never came.

It had been a tough day and Mike and I were exhausted, but our energized hiking partner insisted on climbing toward Cloud's Rest. He led us to a level spot for our sleeping bags just below the tree line. We set up camp and broke out the tequila.

At dinner, we ate more than our fill of pasta, but there were still leftovers.

"I'm not carrying the pasta tomorrow," Mike announced.

Mike and Doug looked at me.

"Let's bury it."

My suggestion brought laughs and agreement.

We buried enough to feed a bear.

Later, as we lay in our sleeping bags, Mike joked his shoulders and back hurt from his heavy pack.

"It will be a lot lighter tomorrow," I said.

That night, I laughed myself to sleep.

There were no cables leading to the top of Cloud's Rest, but I climbed the next morning without incident, except for a brief, dizzying moment when I once again made the mistake of looking over the edge of the trail to the valley floor. When we reached the summit, I struggled to regain the sense of security I felt on Half Dome, which was topped by a flat area the size of a football field. The peak of Cloud's Rest was so narrow I could not escape views of the distant valley floor, threatening my equilibrium. I was afraid Mike and Doug would notice my trembling hands as I gripped my granola bar and camera.

After our snack and photography, we traversed the peak to the other side. I froze when I saw what was ahead: a terrifying ledge about 100 feet long—and not much wider than a backpack—with a sheer, unforgiving drop-off.

I fought to disguise my quickening breaths.

"You okay, Reg?" Doug could tell I was not.

There was nothing to hold onto. One slip and I would die.

"I'll be okay, just give me a minute," I lied. I wanted to turn around and retrace my steps all the way back to Yosemite Valley. Mike reached around his backpack and untied a rope that he had used to hang our food in a tree, out of the reach of bears. His plan was simple, but caught me off guard.

"We can tie ourselves together and we'll crawl on the narrowest parts."

Mike tied the rope around my waist. I eyed the ledge. Doug and Mike looked at me. Their eyes said, "You can do it, Reg."

Doug and Mike could have easily traversed the ledge. I summoned every ounce of grit I could muster and inched, crawled, and shuffled across, tied to my friends. When I visualized the incident later, I knew we must have looked so ridiculous that a video of our effort would have gone viral if YouTube had been on the scene. It didn't occur to me at the time, but if one of us had slipped, we all would have died.

I felt so relieved on the way down Cloud's Rest that I announced, "Careful, it's Reg rock" when I slipped a few more times. Even the eavesdropping squirrels laughed. We rendezvoused with our wives and kids at Tenaya Lake, devoured a late afternoon picnic and motored home. As I drove our Plymouth minivan with Sue to my right and three young sons in the back seats, I felt a supreme sense of accomplishment and gratitude for my backpacking partners.

My peace of mind was short-lived. I had conquered two mountains, but when I arrived home, I destroyed what should have been a great memory. By the time I crawled into bed, I was agonizing over my frozen pasta blunder and the scene at the ledge. How could I have been so careless to agree to the backpacking trip? I had built a life that protected me from exposing my perceived inexperience and weaknesses. Over and over, I had pushed away people who might have discovered my imperfections if I had allowed them inside my world.

The following summer, I told Doug I wasn't up for a backpacking trip because too many guys were going. I didn't believe in my friends nor myself enough to be honest. For 25 years since the Half Dome trek, I missed out on annual backpacking adventures with a group of great guys.

Was I making up excuses again? Was I setting myself up to run from another opportunity, this time to walk the Camino de Santiago with my wife? Were my fears really attached to what happened in a junior high locker room and on a high-country backpacking trip?

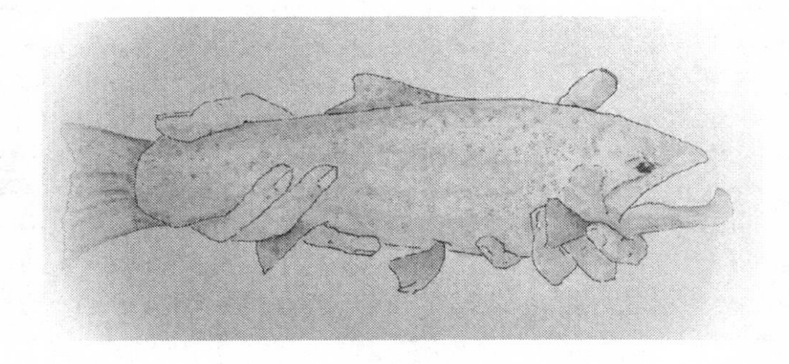

3

What Did the Doctor Say?

On a warm late November morning, I turned my beige Toyota Prius onto the rutted, gravel road. It was about 300 yards to the two-story, wood-sided house where our family had enjoyed tri-tip and chicken barbecues with friends for more than two decades.

The Camino resurfaced over breakfast before I left home and Sue was steadfast in her desire to walk across Spain. I remained reluctant, but that morning I shifted my focus to a commitment with one of my best friends.

My car soon reached the home of Ron and Barbara. Barbara, who was 60, had been a teaching colleague of mine in the Mariposa schools. She carried an unmistakably loud voice, enough energy for a crowd, and the biggest heart in the county. I never heard anyone say anything bad about Ron, 58, her husband. His passion was fishing, but his real loves were Barbara and his daughter Chelsea. Everyone loved Ron, who worked almost all his adult life as a mechanic in Yosemite National Park.

I parked in front of the detached double garage as Ron hobbled out of the side door of his house. He did not look like the same man who could make me appear like a wimp on a mountain trail. As he struggled into his seat, I searched for words. I missed his usual greeting, "Hi Reg," which always came in his gentle, warm tone.

"Good to see you," I said, instead of the usual, "How ya doing, Ron?"

"It was a tough weekend." I hardly recognized his voice.

Ron, who would sacrifice a day of fishing if a friend needed help splitting firewood, was normally energetic and always looked me in the eye when he talked. As I backed the car and pulled onto the gravel road, his eyes were drooped, his arms were limp, and the message was, "Just drive."

Several of us, Ron's retired friends, had been taking turns driving him the 65 miles to Fresno for a variety of doctor and hospital appointments, including chemotherapy. He was fighting the battle of his life. His enemy was leukemia, which had been diagnosed in September. All of us valued the time with our friend, and it allowed Barbara a break so she could go to work.

During the Monday drive to the oncologist, Ron grew slightly more animated as the miles passed. He had been released from the hospital the previous week after another round of chemo. Ron told me the doctor made him promise to monitor his blood pressure and report to Mariposa's Fremont Hospital emergency room if it dropped significantly.

"So, how did you do, Ron?"

"Not so great."

"Did you go to the ER?"

Silence.

Ron had been in St. Agnes Hospital in Fresno several times since the diagnosis so he could be quarantined during chemotherapy and for a few days after each treatment. Breathing masks were required when friends and relatives visited. When he was outside the hospital, he had to wear a mask at all times.

Sue and I brought either Starbucks coffee or a milkshake, two of Ron's favorite treats, when we visited him at the hospital. We left amazed at our friend's positive attitude. We were near-certain leukemia was going to lose the battle.

I steered into the medical office parking lot near St. Agnes Hospital. After a half hour in the oncologist's office, Ron emerged with a request: Starbucks. I could see he was thinking about more than coffee.

Ron peeled away his breathing mask to sip his Verona roast. He chewed a small bite of his muffin.

"What did the doctor say?"

"He said I have to go to St. Agnes for another test." Ron was struggling. Something had happened in the oncologist's office, and I debated if I should ask, but chose to let silence fill the time. We tried to enjoy our coffee and muffins, then made the short drive to the hospital. I entered the St. Agnes parking lot with a few minutes to spare. As we sauntered toward the outpatient area, the double glass door slid open, and a tall, slim nurse who recognized Ron pushed a wheelchair toward us.

"The doctor wants you to go to the emergency room right away."

"Why? What's going on?"

"The blood test results were not good."

"Nooo!" Ron's plea trailed off as he slowly shook his head. He had hoped he would be allowed to return home the same day. I struggled to keep my composure as I processed the news.

The ER waiting room was crowded with about 35 patients, relatives, and friends. After he checked in, I wheeled Ron next to an empty seat and told him I would be right back. I returned to the front desk.

"How soon will my friend see a doctor?"

"I have no idea, sir. As you can see, we are overwhelmed today."

"So is my friend. He is in bad shape."

"We will do the best we can."

Outside, I dialed Woodland School and left a message for Barbara, who returned my call on my way back to the door.

"Reg, can you stay there with him until he sees a doctor?"

"Of course, Barb. I was planning on it."

Over the next several hours, I listened desperately each time the door opened and a nurse appeared, but Ron's name was not called. I don't remember what he and I talked about, but I recall his energy and attitude improved; we even shared a few laughs. His chuckles gave glimpses of the old Ron we all hoped would live many years after he was free of leukemia.

When he was finally wheeled to an examining room late that afternoon, he changed into a hospital gown and lifted himself onto the gurney as a nurse pulled a sheet and blanket over him. There was knock at the door. A cardiologist wearing a long white coat introduced himself.

"The blood test shows reason for concern. We are going to check you into the hospital for more tests." The doctor scratched the top of his head and wrote on the form on his clipboard.

I did not detect a reaction on Ron's face, but it took everything I had to not show mine.

When the doctor left, Ron's eyes showed exhaustion. "You should go home, Reg. You can't do anything here."

"Let me get you some pajamas, Ron." He loathed the skimpy hospital gowns.

I returned from Target with PJs and a treat: Pepperidge Farm Milano cookies. Ron's sweet tooth was still thriving. He had been strong through his nightmare, which was filled with chemotherapy, so much pain, test after test. Yet, here we were, enjoying cookies together. As he chewed, his eyes smiled. I doubted if I could be that resilient.

The door opened and a nurse entered.

"They're ready for you."

As I stood, I searched for words.

I hugged my friend.

"I love you, Ron."

"Me too."

Ron never left the hospital. He died five days later.

More than 200 packed the church for Ron's memorial. His daughter Chelsea organized a slide show, which flashed on the large screen. One photo showed Ron with Chelsea when she was a child; another pictured him backpacking with Doug, Mike, and other friends. A few slides later and it was Ron, Barbara, Sue, and I posing before a backdrop of fall color in the eastern Sierra Nevada. On the day the picture was taken, Ron effortlessly identified trees and plants as well as fish in the stream. At one point, he stopped us and pointed to a spider pulling a dead creature across the trail, then described in intricate detail how the spider built a home. He would have been a great guide or science professor. He regretted not going further in his education. Being a mechanic was a job to him, one he complained about from time to time, especially in recent years.

At 58, leukemia took Ron when he was looking forward to leaving the working world and enjoying life on his own terms. His death reminded me life can be fragile.

As Sue and I sat in our living room a few hours after the memorial, I told her I knew what I was getting her for Christmas.

"And I think you should get me the same thing."

"What's that?"

"A backpack. We're going to walk the Camino."

4

Running Away From Home

A white blanket covered the three acres around our ranch-style Mariposa home Christmas morning as pine tree branches drooped under two inches of fresh snow. Our large living room, with a vaulted, pine ceiling, was toasty, thanks to the glowing fire in the wood stove. Our 24-year-old son Andrew played Santa and delivered gifts to his wife Leah, his brother Brad, 23, his 86-year-old grandpa, and his Uncle Kenny. Our third son, Chris, Brad's twin, was living in West Virginia.

Andrew placed two similar-size packages in front of Sue and me without the "Ho, ho, ho" of the real Santa Claus. I removed the gift wrap and folded it carefully. Since joining our family two years before, Leah had inspired our recycling of wrapping paper.

"Nobody's going to miss seeing you on the trail," Andrew observed as I held the bright red Deuter 40-liter backpack I hoped to carry across Spain in spring. Sue unwrapped her package, revealing another red Deuter pack, 32 liters. Both were carryon size, but mine would expand to 50 liters for food on the trail. I was not sure where Sue would fit her food. (Just kidding.)

Brad lifted my pack with two fingers. "I love these packs; they're light. Dad, I bet even you could carry this." All three of our sons, as well as daughter-in-law Leah, were experienced backpackers.

My acquiescence to walk the Camino set off shopping trips to REI, Eddie Bauer, and Costco. We only had ourselves to support, and we faced no further college expenses for the kids, so we could splurge with new equipment and clothing. No hand-me-downs on this trip.

An REI sales person ticked off backpacking equipment suggestions: bear spray, sleeping pad, cooking stove.

I shook my head. "We won't need any of that."

She scrunched her forehead. "Where are you hiking?"

"The Camino in Spain; we'll have a bed and hot meals every day."

"Oh, sure, I've had other customers do that one."

"I call it slack-packing."

My quip earned a polite chuckle.

We wrapped many of the trekking purchases and put them under the Christmas tree so we would have packages to open. "Oh, honey, you shouldn't have," we joked to each other as we opened several gifts we had bought together.

I was 60, and Sue was 55 when we retired earlier in 2012. I taught political science at the Madera Community College campus, and Sue sold newspaper advertising for the Sierra Star in Oakhurst. We could live on my teaching pension, plus our future Social Security benefits. We would use our savings for big trips.

We felt fortunate to be able to retire early, but it was not an easy decision, mainly because we both still liked our jobs. Our sons were living on their own, so leaving home was almost as easy as locking the front door. We craved more freedom, especially the ability to travel in the offseason.

Before watching *The Way*, our idea of adventure was a week in New York City with few plans. We spent more time wandering the streets of Manhattan and sipping coffee at cafes than exploring the halls of the Metropolitan Museum. We sat outside the Met, dining on hot dogs from a cart, rather than carving chateaubriand in the Rainbow Room at the Rockefeller Center. Sue and I were unconventional travelers.

We had both struggled with health issues that made it clear that life could change in an instant. But we were in excellent health, one benefit of regular exercise. And the extra weight would be in our backpacks, not around our waists. I stood six-foot-one, Sue five-foot-six, and some still referred to us as skinny, a term we found anything but endearing.

After the Christmas holiday, we worked off the pie calories through practice day hikes around our neighborhood and Yosemite National Park. On the morning of our first practice, we spread out our equipment and clothing on our bed. Outside, a thin layer of snow remained.

"Are we going to try the trekking poles today?" Sue asked.

Some hikers around Yosemite used them, but most of those people were older than us. Plus, we told each other that trekkers with poles were wimps.

"Twenty years from now, that'll be us," I said once after passing a couple with trekking poles on the Four-Mile Trail in Yosemite. However, after reading an online forum recommendation, we bought two inexpensive sets at Costco.

"Let's see what the guidebook says." Sue looked up trekking poles in the Camino de Santiago guidebook by John Brierley that had just arrived via Amazon.

"He recommends them and says we should use two to avoid being lopsided."

"I'm already lopsided," I joked as I pranced around the room with one pole that I pretended to use as a cane. Sue ignored my attempt at humor, as my family had learned to do over the years.

"I think we should try them. How long should they be?"

I consulted Professor YouTube, who advised to adjust them slightly so they would be shorter than elbow height for flat surfaces, even shorter for uphill, and longer for downhill. We adjusted our poles for flat ground, watched the video again to see how to strap them onto our wrists and put them aside so we could pack.

I rolled up my clothes and squeezed them into extra-large Ziploc bags, sitting on each one to force out the air before zipping it shut. Underwear and socks in one, shirts in another, trousers and shorts in a third bag. Moisture-wicking materials dominated. I stuffed my rain gear in the bottom pocket of my pack. My backpacking sleeping bag and sleeping liner fit in the bottom of the main compartment. Basic toiletries filled another bag; I didn't sit on that one. Our first aid kit, filled with plastic blister patches and other blister treatments, slipped into the top flap.

It was time for a weigh-in. We read that novices should keep their packs close to 10 percent of their body weight.

I stepped on the scale: 165 pounds. I climbed on the scale again, this time wearing my pack: 186. Add about two pounds for water, a 23-pound load. Sue weighed in at 110, 129 with her loaded backpack. That would be about 21 pounds with water, almost double the recommendation.

"I am either going to go naked or without sleeping and rain gear."

"Or we devour pizza, pasta, and pie five times a day," I suggested. "I don't think you have time to double your weight before we leave, though."

"I would probably *lose* weight." Sue rolled her eyes.

We each pulled on thin wool socks followed by a thicker pair, laced up our waterproof Merrell hiking shoes and donned our lightweight down First Ascent jackets. My tight-fitting coat was black; Sue's was purple. We hoisted our backpacks onto our shoulders, buckled up, and squeezed two filled water bottles into pockets on the sides of our packs. The chilly winter air greeted us when we stepped outside.

We had walked about half an hour in our rural, forested neighborhood about 13 miles south of Mariposa when Mary and Sean turned into their driveway just ahead of us in their blue Honda SUV.

Mary stood with her hands on her hips and faced us as if she was about to give a lecture.

"What are you two doing? Are you sure you can handle all the weight on your back, Reg?"

"Running away from home! Can you feed our cat?" I replied. "We're getting in shape for the Camino."

"What's that?" wondered Sean, who preferred fishing over trekking, or over almost anything.

"It's a 500-mile pilgrimage across northern Spain," I answered.

"Five hundred miles? Do you really think you can do that?" Mary laughed. "You don't look like pilgrims."

"Sue thinks we can. I'll probably take a bus."

That finally got a smile out of Sean.

Sue and I related a few more serious details about the trek and continued on our way.

I chuckled at Mary's questions, but her joke about how much I could carry echoed. Little did she know. I lugged plenty of extra baggage that I feared would reveal itself to fellow pilgrims.

Anxiety had chased me like a rabid dog most of my life. Its bite was more painful than Eddie's snapping towel. My brain routinely turned minor problems into catastrophes. A doctor prescribed medication, but it made me feel like a zombie, so I quit taking it. In my early fifties, I finally connected with a counselor, a weathered Vietnam veteran. I told him things I never considered telling two other therapists, even after months of meetings. I had at least a year's worth of couch stories that were bursting to get out. He showed me his disfigured arm, which had barely survived a Vietnam battle. We embraced after our first session. He dropped dead a few days later. I was devastated.

My cardiologist agreed that my mental struggles may have caused my chronic atrial fibrillation that led to open heart surgery. But unless they noticed my chewed fingers and fidgeting, I hid the extent of my anxiety from friends and most family. Mom was aware I was troubled, but her knowledge only scratched the surface. When my crying awakened her in the middle of the night, she sat on my bed, held my hand, and advised, "Stop being such a worry wart." But, even with Mom, I made up stories to cover most of the details of my problems at school. I never told her about kids who thought it was hysterical when I flinched or ducked at their fake punches. My greatest fear was that one day, the punch would not be a fake. Why did kids think it was so funny to throw a ball at me, yell, "Spittle, catch!" as the ball hit me in the chest or stomach? Probably because I doubled over as I tried to catch my breath. Also, I never asked Mom why Dad was so distant and sad, or why he favored Joe over me.

Ultimately, painful events in my life hurt the people I loved the most: Sue and my sons Andrew, Brad, and Chris.

I fought my habit that would make the Camino another place for worry. The trek would force me to learn new things. I was afraid I'd stand out as a rookie trekker, like the new kid in class.

My other voice fought for attention.

"Reg, you're 60, not 13! There will be plenty of other newbies. They will be thinking about themselves, not you!"

The walk promised to deliver numerous surprises. The journey would take me places I never imagined and expose ghosts that had been dormant for decades. And I had not considered the opportunities that Camino relationships would bring to my life. No matter how much I practiced in California, I would be unprepared for what was going to take place in Spain.

Sue and I knew physical practice was a good idea. Over the next several months, we walked five or six miles at a time around our hilly neighborhood, carrying our packs, usually using trekking poles. We walked at least two or three times a week and made several one-hour drives to Yosemite for treks as long as 12 miles. Wearing my backpack, I sometimes felt out of place as people passed by on the roads. Most ignored us, but some pedestrians stopped and asked what we were doing. Many were intrigued by the Camino.

On a springlike day in March, we set out for a practice hike in Yosemite. I parked our Prius near Yosemite Village and, as I climbed out, I was struck by a painful reminder as I looked across the parking lot. I stared at the huge garage with several folding vertical doors large enough to fit a bus. It was the shop where Ron had worked. Leukemia had been like a lightning bolt, taking one of the strongest men I knew in less than three months. It still didn't seem possible.

I remembered the voices of his many coworkers who honored him at his memorial as I turned and began the 12-mile loop around Yosemite Valley. We had traveled several miles through the pine forest beneath El Capitan, the massive, sheer rock face, when a couple who were old enough to have watched first-run *Lassie* episodes as kids approached from the other direction. They wore daypacks and stepped at a leisurely pace.

"Where are you two coming from?" asked Vic, raising his bushy black eyebrows.

"Oh, we're just doing the valley loop ..."

"But why are you carrying backpacks?"

Sue told them a little about the Camino. "We're trying to get our old bodies ready."

Wendy, Vic's hiking partner, adjusted her daypack. "I wish we were younger and in good enough shape to do that."

"Lots of people older than us walk the Camino." I wanted to encourage them.

"But I'm not sure I could lug a backpack over that distance." Vic's reservations sounded familiar.

"There are companies that will transport your luggage from village to village for you." I tried not to sound like a travel agent.

Wendy and Vic had recently retired and were taking their rented RV on a spring trip around California.

"We're experimenting with the motorhome life," Vic said.

"How do you like it?" I asked.

"Well," he scratched the side of his neck.

"We got a 24-footer from CruiseAmerica, and it's too big. I liked pulling our tent trailer better; I could see over it in the rear view mirror."

Vic's story took me back to the tent trailer we owned for five years. One family trip came six weeks after I had open-heart surgery to repair what Vincent Gaudiani, my doctor, called an electrical problem. We visited Yellowstone and Grand Tetons National Parks on our way to the Black Hills and Mount Rushmore. Dr. God, as he was called by many of his heart surgery patients, cleared me for the trip but forbid any lifting.

Andrew was 13 at the time and Brad and Chris were 11. All three had inherited Sue's and my thin frames, but were stronger than they looked. They were all at home in any athletic competition, especially basketball and soccer.

"So, Dad, I think heart surgery was a pretty lame move to get you out of all this work," Chris joked. He cranked up the fiberglass tent trailer roof while his brothers set up the tent Andrew would use that night near the Grand Tetons.

"I'm still pretty weak." Actually, I was feeling almost back to normal.

"More like a weakling."

"Where's the respect?" I put my hands over my chest and feigned pain.

"Same place as the truth." Chris was quick.

All the kids loved camping, especially Brad, who lobbied unsuccessfully to live in the tent trailer parked in our front yard. Travel with Sue and the boys dominate my highlight reel of fatherhood.

After wishing Wendy and Vic many more retirement adventures, we continued our Yosemite trek, stopping for a short picnic next to a creek. We finally returned to Yosemite Village about 4 p.m.

"Twelve miles, five and a half hours," Sue reported after checking her wristwatch and the mileage counter that was strapped to her ankle.

"Almost like a full day on the Camino," she added. We had allowed six weeks for the trip, including travel days to and from Madrid, and several rest days. We would need to average 15 miles a day to complete the 500 miles.

My shoulders were sore, but the pack had begun to feel like part of me. I wondered how it would feel after five weeks. I had not experienced a middle-of-the-night panic attack for a couple of weeks, but my worries about the trek lurked. Would there be a way to steal some privacy in the dorms and bathrooms? Sue said no one would want to have a look-see anyway. She probably had that right. I wondered if I would remember to pack my sense of humor.

April 8 came quickly, and I squeezed the Ziploc bags and other equipment into my backpack for the final time before our flight out of Fresno the next day. Sue had already loaded her backpack into the car. We packed the trekking poles in a box so we could check them at the airport; we had read they would not pass security if they were attached to our packs.

My coming adventure paled in comparison to my parents' moves from Great Britain to Montreal, Canada as children with their large families. Their ocean liner crossings had to have been trying. Neither family had much money, so they were crammed into lower-deck rooms. No balconies, no swimming pools, nor all-you-can-eat buffets.

My father was 51, and my mother was 37 when I was born in Seattle, the first American-born child on either side of the family.

Dad, who stood five-four and weighed less than most high school freshmen boys, was an unconventional father. He didn't talk to me much, never played catch, and never seemed content as he moved our family countless times across the country, across the county, or across town. I don't remember ever getting close enough to detect the cigarette smell on his clothes. My younger brother Joe did, though, when he sat in Dad's lap at the kitchen table. I had longed to feel my father's arms around me.

Mom, who was two inches taller than Dad and carried a larger frame, was the anchor in my life. Smoking and diet would catch up with her in later years, but she was physically strong when I was a kid. Her expressive eyes and loving touch were antidotes for my distress. When I was in junior high school, I occasionally sneaked a cigarette from the wooden box she kept by her bedside, and I smoked it far away from our trailer park. I was mortified when she told me one Saturday, "You shouldn't smoke, Reggie." I hated to disappoint her—ever.

As I examined my pricey trekking clothing and gear, I remembered how Mom squeezed every penny out of each dollar. She worked six days a week cleaning hospital rooms and people's houses at minimum wage so she could feed and clothe Joe and me. Most of my clothes were used and out of style. My pants would have stayed dry in a flood. At the time, I hated most of them and sometimes resented Mom for making me wear them, especially when I went to school.

When I was seven, we moved to New Hampshire in our 16-foot olive green travel trailer towed by a 1952 green Nash four-door.

That winter, snow covered the trailer while we lived in a tiny cottage. As a second-grader, I waited in subfreezing temperatures for the mini school bus, which followed the snowplow to take me to the 12-grade schoolhouse. There was no kindergarten for Joe, so I used a chalkboard to teach the alphabet to my brother, an eager student.

We moved back to Seattle the next year. About 12 months later, we moved to Southern California in the same 16-footer, again pulled by the Nash. We had lived in the trailer for about a year when my dad moved us into an aging, aluminum-sided 50-foot-by-8-foot mobile home with louvered windows. That home took us to four trailer parks around Ventura County in four years. Dad would sometimes chauffeur my mom, who didn't drive, to her cleaning jobs, but she often took a bus while he sat at the small dining table as I left for school. He would usually be there when I got home, but he had a beer in front of him instead of a cup of tea. I hid out in my refuge, a pint-sized bedroom at the back of the trailer, until my mom got home from work. As an adult, painful scars from my mobile childhood have surfaced in ways I have struggled to understand.

The person who sat at our trailer's dining table wasn't at all like any of the fathers I saw at other boys' homes. I don't remember him ever having a job; his seventh-grade education limited his options. On the rare occasion when a childhood friend saw him, I dreaded the question: "Is that your grandpa?"

Mom lived long enough to see me finish college, marry, have children, and buy a home. She didn't go beyond tenth grade, but I am pretty sure I was a baby in her arms when she first told me I would go to college.

I eyed my Camino backpack on the bed one more time. Something was missing. It was the small LED flashlight we had bought for nighttime trips to the albergue bathrooms. I found it on the living room side table and turned back toward the hall leading to our bedroom. I paused in the hallway, where we hung family photographs, and contemplated the picture of my newlywed parents. When Dad died at 73, I was a senior at the University of California at Santa Barbara, and I felt little emotion at his funeral. I weighed what I passed on to my children and recognized something I got from Dad: his wanderlust. Perhaps that was pulling me to Spain.

I tucked the flashlight into the pouch in the top of my pack, pulled the drawstring tightly and fastened the buckles. As I carried my pack to the car, I stopped again at my parents' photograph and smiled at Mom, who died in 1997 at 82.

"I'm going for a walk, Mom. See you when I get back."

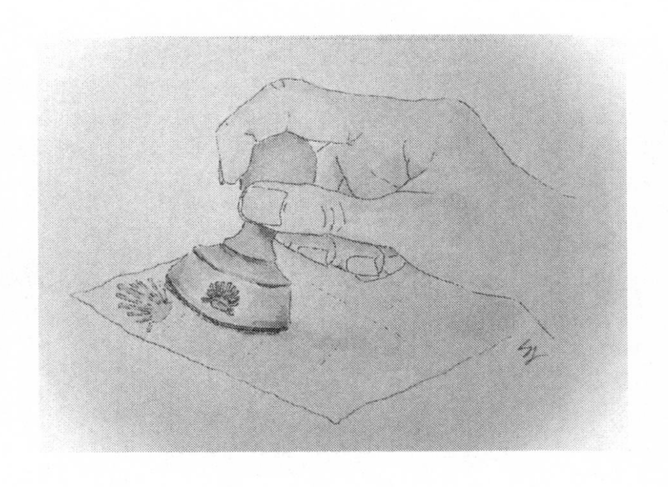

5

You Are Officially Pilgrims

I stuffed our red backpacks into the overhead compartment for the second leg of our overnight flight from Dallas to Madrid. A flight attendant approached; her high heels almost elevated her to my height.

"Are you walking the Camino?" she asked while eyeing our packs.

"Yes, we are," I replied, looking at Sue, who had taken her seat in the middle of the cramped economy section of the jumbo jet, leaving me the aisle.

"You are going to love it!"

Another member of the flight crew stopped next to me.

"They are doing the Camino," said the first attendant.

"We did it together last year," she added, pointing her thumb toward her colleague.

As other passengers watched us curiously, the two women agreed they would do the trek again. I was confident they would be strong walkers.

"Come with us!" I offered.

"Oh, I wish we could." They smiled, turned, and hurried to the front of the plane to prepare for takeoff.

I still had trouble believing I was going to attempt the Camino de Santiago, but the flight attendants' spotlight made it seem less surreal. Their enthusiasm excited me, but I also knew they were almost 20 years younger.

As we settled into our seats, I pulled out my iPad and ear buds, tools to keep my palms dry. My playlist included favorites Snow Patrol, Mat Kearney, Fun and James Blunt. This time, the music battled more than sweaty palms and turbulence, while I confronted my checklist of perceived inadequacies. I closed my eyes and focused on the rhythms of my breathing and the music.

Later, as we ate dinner (deli sandwiches from the Dallas airport) we skimmed the first few stages in the Brierley guidebook. This was our first European trip without reservations, with the exception of our opening-night booking in Pamplona. According to our online research, it was unnecessary to book rooms or beds, except sometimes during the summer. Many stages (a stage is one day of trekking) featured villages and accommodations every three to five miles, so we thought we could stop when we got tired or when we found an irresistible place. We would be in Spain six weeks, all but one night without reservations. In a matter of hours and throughout the journey, our flexibility would be tested.

I snapped awake when the plane began its descent into Madrid. Groggy passengers stretched and looked out the windows as we touched down gently on a sunny morning. I laced up my Merrells as we taxied to the gate. When the seat belt sign flicked off, adrenaline jolted my body. I tugged our backpacks from the overhead compartment and, for the first of what would be scores of times in Spain, we hoisted them onto our shoulders. As we filed past the crew, the flight attendants we had talked to the night before greeted us with two words that would become so familiar: "Buen Camino!"

Minutes later we stood at the Madrid Airport luggage carousel with 200 other passengers and watched bags clunk down the conveyor belt. But, after 20 minutes, the belt stopped moving and our box containing our trekking poles was absent. We searched other carousels and could not find anyone to help us. After an hour, exhausted and frustrated, we found our lonely box with our poles in the oversized baggage area. We called it Camino lesson number one: Never give up.

With the trekking poles strapped to our packs, we lifted them onto our backs and buckled up. I remembered the first time Tom, in *The Way,* wore his son's backpack and began his trek. The town's police chief yelled to him and pointed across the bridge. Tom had gone the wrong way. Like Tom, I had a lot to learn. I hoped someone would be there for me when I needed direction.

Our first stop was the Orange store to buy an international SIM card for Sue's iPhone. My Spanish did not include much phone terminology, but, luckily, the store clerk's English reached far enough to explain how the card worked as he installed the tiny chip. He loaded enough time for emergencies and calls to check accommodations on the trail.

It was mid-afternoon when we found the bus terminal outside the airport after buying snacks at a convenience store. We held two tickets to Pamplona, in northeastern Spain, that we had bought at a kiosk in the airport. Two buses would take more than five hours to deliver us to the city famous for the annual running of the bulls. The buses were tall, with high back seats, big windows, and plenty of leg room. I heard only Spanish on both buses—when I was awake. There were several families with small children. I slept two or three hours, making up for some of the sleep I missed on the cramped, noisy, bumpy plane.

It was dark when our bus pulled into the Pamplona terminal where several other buses were unloading or loading passengers. The driver lifted our backpacks from the compartment on the underside of the bus.

"Buen Camino!" came with his warm smile.

Hungry, tired, and longing for showers after 25 hours of travel, we scanned a busy intersection in the bustling city of 200,000 and searched for street signs that would guide us. Our albergue reservation had been canceled via an e-mail, which told us the proprietor had rented out the entire place to a group. I had a few choice words for her when we got the note, but at least she found us an alternative room in a small pensión, an inexpensive hotel.

It seemed like cheating to take a taxi to our pensión, so we walked. It was one of many times when we would be thankful for

John Brierley's guidebook, which held a map of Pamplona. I worried that the pensión may not have received our reservation.

"The door is locked, and I don't see any lights." Sue heard the frustration in my voice as we stood outside the Pensión el Camino. I asked myself if we would spend the night in our sleeping bags on the plaza bench we had just passed.

"Here, look at this." Sue pointed to a sign next to the pensión door.

I punched in the phone number and was confused when a deep, loud voice answered in Irish-accented English. As he talked, a light flashed from the second floor (or first floor, in European terms), a window opened, and a man holding a phone to his ear leaned out and waved.

"Welcome to Pamplona! I'll be right down."

Appearing like he would be at home among wild soccer fans in an Irish pub, he opened the door and presented Sue with his business card.

"Hello, I'm Mr. Pamplona! Right this way!"

Sue and I caught each other's surprised expressions that said, "What's an Irishman doing in Spain calling himself Mr. Pamplona?"

He led us up the dark, narrow stairway to a room littered with stacks of papers and boxes.

"Passports, please," Mr. Pamplona requested as he pointed at two wooden chairs next to his cluttered desk. How did he get the title? I was too tired to ask, but I imagined it could have been the result of a body-building contest when he was younger. Or perhaps it was self-bestowed.

The muscle man opened our American passports and our *Credenciales del Peregrino* (Pilgrim passports), wallet-size pieces of thin cardboard, which unfolded into a strip more than two feet wide. We had learned through a forum online that the Camino passports would be required at all accommodations, so we had ordered them through the American Pilgrims on the Camino website a few months before.

Mr. Pamplona pulled a small rubber stamp with a short handle from his desk drawer, dabbed it on an ink pad, and pounded a blue scallop shell next to the words "Pensión el Camino," in our passports. He wrote the date next to the stamp and announced, "You are officially pilgrims!" The passport stamping would become one of many daily routines that would mark our lives during the weeks ahead.

Although his act might get old quickly, I was happy we found Mr. Pamplona. I realized another lesson as I took a deep breath, feeling my tension ease: Stay flexible. I gave him two twenty-euro bills. The euro was trading for about $1.30, meaning our room cost about $52. He led us a few steps to our small, bare room with a double bed. Normally I would have declared, "This place is a dump!" but that night I was thankful we had a room. My mood improved even more when I saw the en suite bathroom with a shower. Our Irish host told us a bar across the street served late meals if we were hungry. In just 15 minutes, we had gone from the possibility of sleeping on a bench to a bed, shower, and a hot meal. I could have hugged Mr. Pamplona with my bony arms, but settled on, "Thank you very much!"

We unpacked, showered, and stepped into the crisp evening. Nervous energy fueled our pace and heightened our appetites as we crossed the narrow street and ate while seated at the bar. Soccer fans watched a match on television and cheered, drank, yelled, cussed, and drank some more. I sipped a tall, cold glass of frothy lager and chewed a bite of the largest sausage I had ever eaten. It was the first of countless Spanish bars for us. We were beat, but we loved it.

Welcome to Pamplona. Welcome to Spain. Welcome to the Camino de Santiago.

6

I Heard a Cry of Pain

Neither of us had slept well in the Pamplona pensión. It might have been jet lag or our excitement for the first steps of our Camino after months of anticipation. Within minutes of awakening, news from the mountains presented an unexpected dilemma.

Spring had been an obvious choice for us to walk the Camino Francés, another name for the path that began just over the border in France. Spring would be less crowded and cooler than summer and we preferred green fields and wildflowers to fall color and brown hillsides. We forecasted the second week of April would give us a good chance to avoid snow.

The news proved us wrong. A snowstorm had closed the Pyrenees Mountain pass above the usual starting point, St. Jean Pied de Port, France. The 43-mile climb and descent through the Pyrenees to Pamplona was one of the toughest sections, but I didn't want an asterisk attached to our trek. It could be days before the pass reopened. I was battling my linear inner voice, which focused on connecting the start to the finish.

We sat up in bed and debated our choices. Do we take the €100 taxi to St. Jean as we planned? But the alternative path from St. Jean included long sections on or next to a road on its way to Pamplona. We worried about traffic and the risk of injury if we encountered snow or ice.

"We should just start here in Pamplona." At first, I rejected the idea, but I knew Sue was right. We needed to focus on what was important: the journey. Still, we were disappointed. Our decision would affect virtually everything for the next five weeks, for better or worse.

The time had come to load up our backpacks, eat breakfast, and find our way out of the city. We were entering a world of unknowns. I would have been even more nervous had I known more about what the night would bring. A five-minute stroll in the chilly morning air delivered us to the Plaza del Castillo, about 100 yards square, where we found a busy bar with a line of several customers. Fresh baked goods filled a glass case, and an orange juice machine was perched behind the counter. Whole oranges waited atop the contraption, which automatically squeezed juice from them into a glass. The machines were a common feature of the bars across Spain. I smelled strong coffee from the espresso machine. There were no eggs, bacon, and hash browns and no coffee pot with unlimited refills, but it was not a breakfast joint in California.

I studied the menu and tried to listen to people ahead of me order their breakfast, but they spoke so fast that I could only understand small parts. I was determined to order in Spanish without pointing. I exchanged "*Buenos días*" (good morning) greetings with the fast-working man in front of the espresso machine. Then "*por favor*," (please) followed by: "*Dos cafés con leche*, (two espressos with frothy hot milk), *dos zumos de naranja* (two orange juices), and *dos croissants*. I held up two fingers for each item just in case. Sue winced at my pronunciation, but I was pleased that all I wanted ended up on a tray. I figured there was a good chance the server would have preferred that I had spoken in English. I used a €20 note to pay the €8 bill, saying, "*Muchas gracias*" as I picked up the tray. We had read we would need cash for some accommodations and stores, especially in smaller villages, so we brought €300 that we ordered through our local bank to get us started. ATMs along the Camino would replenish our cash.

A small table next to the window hosted our first breakfast in Spain. The croissant was buttery and fresh. The orange juice was thick with pulp. I sipped the strong coffee that I had been craving all morning and listened to four short, gray-haired men at the next table chatter in Spanish and wondered if they came to the bar every day. They were talking too fast for me to understand more than a few words. I was getting a taste of Spain, and I liked it.

Sue and I considered a second croissant and another coffee, but we chose not to keep the Camino waiting. The guidebook led us a block north of the plaza to the Camino de Santiago, where yellow arrows, stripes, scallop shells, and even dots would be our beacons. They appeared on walls, posts, rocks, tree trunks, just about anywhere, usually in plain sight.

As I followed the scallop shells imbedded in the sidewalk, fast-moving pedestrians left me in their wake. Other than Sue, there was not another backpacker in sight. I wore trekking clothes and a wide-brimmed hat while carrying my jam-packed red backpack next to crowds of people going about their daily lives. My pack felt good, my shoes felt right, but I felt out of place. I didn't feel like a pilgrim. I had retained my childhood sensitivity when I perceived I wasn't fitting in, and my usual response was to withdraw. Here, in Pamplona, as I had feared, there was nowhere to hide. Just minutes into the trek, and I hoped comfort would be around the corner.

Sue paused to photograph flowers at a neatly groomed park brimming with shade trees and lush grass. We planned a WordPress blog post every afternoon or evening. Sue's photography would anchor our posts. After skirting a university, we bought energy bars at a small market. A long wooden bench outside of the city next to the trail was a perfect place for a break, even though we had only come two or three miles. The rural scene mirrored the Camino I had expected to see.

As we unwrapped chocolate-covered energy bars, a dark-haired woman just past high school age dropped her pack on the end of the bench. She greeted us in what sounded like an Australian accent and pulled rain gear and plastic food containers from her large backpack. I waited for her to lift out a red-and-white checkered tablecloth and a bottle of wine, but they never appeared.

"I think my pack is unbalanced," she explained. "This is my first day, and my shoulders hurt already."

Damn. I thought she was going to share a picnic with us.

As we ate our snack, she repacked her backpack, buckled it shut, hoisted it onto her shoulders, and was gone with a cheerful, "Buen Camino!"

"Now I also have to worry about my pack being unbalanced." Sue smiled, rolled her eyes, and shook her head. "Geez."

The path zigzagged in large swaths like it was climbing to the sky, but it was Alto del Perdón, a 2,590-foot mountain pass far in the distance. After about an hour and a half of steady, but not steep, climbing we came around yet another corner and found a tiny, stone-walled store with a handful of trekkers sitting on an ancient-looking rock wall. Their sandwiches were wrapped in white paper, like they had come from the store.

"Hola!" said a bearded hiker, with a mouthful of lunch.

"How are the sandwiches?" I asked the group. A couple of thumbs up signs, and the bearded guy said, "The best within miles!" as he surveyed the grain-covered landscape with no other building in sight. I was hungry again already. Was it the hiking, outdoors, or nervous energy?

Within minutes, Sue and I joined the group on the wall with our cheese sandwiches. As I chewed hungrily, I observed the other trekkers' backpacks, some leaning against the wall and others lying on the ground. Several hikers had shed their boots as they laughed and shared stories under clouds that drifted by in the light, cool breeze. My legs swung back and forth. The cheese was tasty, the bread was fresh. I had discovered the Camino's tranquility.

The talkative trekker with the beard lifted his black pack, swaggered over to us and asked where in America we came from.

"California, near Yosemite," I answered.

"Best state in America! What movie stars do you know?" Beaton asked as he wiped his nose with the back of his hand.

"We live a long way from Hollywood," I said.

His disappointment showed.

"But I once belonged to the same health club as John Travolta."

He winked and nodded. "I could use some California sunshine. We see the sun almost every week in London."

Beaton and our other lunch companions departed with a "Buen Camino," leaving us sitting outside the store. Beaton was the only one to adjust his poles to make them shorter for the uphill. I guessed he saw the same YouTube video I watched. One tall, husky trekker held just one pole in his right hand at shoulder level and pounded it firmly into the ground as he walked. I could feel the shoulder pain he faced, which he could have avoided if he had watched Professor YouTube.

I was pleased how friendly people had been at our stops. The trail had been mostly wide and easy so far. That was about to change. The track became slightly steeper as it led us toward Alto del Perdón, also known as the Hill of Forgiveness. Our trekking poles soon proved their worth, steadying us as we stepped gingerly around sticky mud several inches thick, bordered by soggy tall grass. I leaned on the pole in my right hand and stepped along the grassy slope to my left, above the mud, which showed many skids of hikers who had slipped. Large rocks added to the challenge.

Sue paused to plan her route around a wide mucky stretch. "We would be a muddy mess without poles."

It was a slow, difficult hour before we reached the wind-blown pass. I snapped Sue's picture next to the *peregrino* (pilgrim) monument, featuring taller-than-life flat iron sculptures of pilgrims representing different eras of the Camino. Suddenly, I heard a cry of pain behind me from a burly guy in his twenties who was sitting on a waist-high rock, wincing as he examined his swollen knee. A woman about his age helped him wrap it with an elastic bandage as tears streamed down his cheeks. "If he is in such bad shape so early, how will two old folks like us do?" I wondered.

I pulled the guidebook from a back pocket of Sue's pack to check our progress.

"We've done about seven miles, a mile less than halfway," I told Sue. We had hoped to reach Puente la Reina, but there were two other villages on the way with albergues.

"What's this red exclamation point mean?" The guidebook answered my question: Watch for loose, slippery rocks on the way down the mountain. Before beginning the steep descent, we surveyed the valley below, where the Camino path twisted between green fields. Snow-capped peaks provided background contrast.

Black clouds closed in as we measured our steps down the mountain. I didn't remember Martin Sheen encountering such large rocks, or negotiating steep downhill sections. Several trekkers barely old enough to buy beer zoomed by, leaping from the top of one large rock to the other, as if they were skiing from one mogul to the next. "Buen Camino!" they cheered without a tinge of sarcasm. I slowly stepped down sideways from one rock they had leaped over. I almost fell when the weight of my pack shifted.

We had traveled nine miles from Pamplona when we approached a courtyard next to the Camino del Perdón, a private albergue in the small village of Uterga. Seven or eight people sat at outdoor tables that held beers or coffees. Their backpacks were lined up at the wall leading to the door, saving a place for a bed when the albergue office opened.

"Hola! Come on in!" one woman said, waving. There was Beaton, who shouted, "There are the Californians!"

We walked along our red-carpet welcome to the small, two-story building, bought two *cafés con leche* at the small bar, and sat at a covered table outside. Beaton nodded at me from the next table, where he talked loudly to two men about half his age who soon stood up, slipped on their backpacks, and announced they were rushing off to try to beat the rain to the next village.

"Hold on, blokes! I'm goin' wit ya." Beaton scrambled to catch up.

I sipped my coffee as it started to rain. Everyone rushed to move their backpacks under cover. I expected Beaton and his companions to return to get out of the rain, but they must have braved it. We would not see Beaton again.

The front door of the albergue swung open, and the woman who had made our coffees waved, a signal that the hostel was ready for pilgrims.

“We should stay here,” Sue suggested as I considered the alternative, which would require rain gear and either four more miles to Óbanos or almost seven miles to Puente la Reina.

The end of our walking day was about to become a new beginning.

7

Why Can't I Do That?

We retrieved our backpacks, stepped through the front door and unfolded our passports on the counter at the Camino del Perdón, our first albergue. The reception desk doubled as a bar for ordering drinks; several small tables with chairs lined a wide hallway to a dining room in the back.

The long-haired woman was businesslike as she stamped our passports and told us in English it would cost €10 each for a bed and €10 for the three-course pilgrim meal at 6 p.m. For the equivalent of $52, we would both have dinner and a place to sleep. Our host alerted us that the albergue had neither a kitchen nor breakfast. We would pay for missing the significance of her message.

The steep stairway to our first bunk room twice turned sharply to the right, leading to a small common lounge. My throat tightened with each step. I paused when I saw the door leading to the dormitory, inhaled deeply, and reasoned: "This is not a junior high locker room, nor another new classroom."

I slowly opened the door and stepped inside the dimly lit room. Two backpacks occupied bunk beds to my left, where there were six sets of bunks squeezed in rows so close to each other that one could hold hands with the person in the next bed. A woman in one top bunk napped. The room was smaller than I expected for 18 trekkers.

"Those must be taken," Sue whispered, pointing to the bunks with packs.

The woman at the reception desk had warned us we would have to split up if there were no empty bunks together.

"We can't do that!" I had barely stopped short of saying it aloud.

There was one empty bunk straight ahead and two more to our right, next to a small window, the only natural light in the room. "Let's take these," Sue suggested, pointing to the right side.

Sue put her pack on the top bunk, and I took the bunk below. Each bed had a bottom sheet and a blanket. I felt like the nervous new boarder in a summer camp for kids, but I was relieved Sue would be my bunkmate.

"I need to use the bathroom."

"Me too," Sue said.

I relaxed slightly when I spotted two gender-labeled bathroom doors. At the sink, I found a dark-haired man barely a third my age washing his face. Mud clung to the lower legs of his pants. He paused long enough to offer "Hola!" I returned his greeting and slipped through an open door to a tiny room with a toilet. My hands were trembling so much I had trouble unzipping my shorts. It was at least half a minute before I could pee. Outside the toilet room, I saw a plastic curtain that I pulled aside, revealing a small shower room with enough space to change clothes. My body would survive at least another day before being exposed.

The guy I saw in the bathroom stood next to the bunk opposite ours, emptying his pack, which was on the upper bed.

"I'm Alejandro, from Barcelona." He wore a long-sleeve shirt and hiking pants, but I had the impression he was not an experienced backpacker.

"I'm Reg, from California."

"Where did you begin your Camino?" he asked.

"Pamplona. This is our first day."

"I am on a break from my job. I hope I can make it to Burgos in 10 days, when I have to go back to work. Are you going to Santiago?"

"I hope so. Are you here on your own?"

He nodded. "I was nervous about doing this by myself, but it feels like a friendly place so far."

As I considered the young Spaniard who had been extra friendly, I knew I would not be here without a trekking partner. Alejandro's courage matched his command of English. But he was not afraid to admit he was nervous. Why can't I do that?

I introduced Sue when she returned.

"I wish I had shoes like yours." Alejandro pointed to our Merrells on the floor under the window. "My shoes are terrible. I slipped in the mud on the hill." I glanced at his mud-caked Adidas sneakers on the floor as he returned to unpacking. I remembered my two-day Yosemite backpacking trip in similar shoes, when I slipped many times and fell hard once.

Sue had climbed the ladder to the top bunk and lay with her head propped against her inflated REI pillow. She had logged onto Wi-Fi and was checking e-mail.

I opened my pack, pulled out the plastic bags, and dug out a change of clothes. I grabbed my toiletries bag.

"I think I'll take a shower."

"The room is nice, don't you think?" Sue sought a sign that I was comfortable. "Does your shower have enough room to change clothes?"

I glanced behind me to see if Alejandro had heard Sue's questions. "It's fine," I said, through my clenched teeth, rolling my eyes.

Craig, my high school best friend, would have replied differently.

I could hear his answer. "No, there's no room to undress in the shower. I'll just strip here; it's no big deal, right?" And everyone would have laughed. Craig always made everything look so easy.

As I undressed behind the plastic shower curtain, I remembered that my worst-case scenarios rarely mimicked reality. Alejandro had been quick to offer welcoming words. It didn't matter to him I was almost 40 years older. As I basked in the soothing shower, I rinsed away my fears, at least for the moment.

After we finished sprucing up, more backpacks occupied bunks in the dorm, and several trekkers sat on beds, talking. It was stuffy, so I opened the window next to our bunk. We hung our small, damp backpacking towels on the ends of our beds and descended the steep stairs to the bar.

The older of two men in the bar invited us to join them at a table for four. Sue and I brought our glasses of Tempranillo wine, a regional specialty. At first glance, I saw a drawing of a pistol on Hal's red t-shirt, but a closer look revealed a small map of Florida. I chuckled at my mistake, but kept it to myself. I figured Hal was near retirement age. Clement, who parted his thick dark hair down the middle, was less than half way there. I doubted that they were trekking partners; probably just having drinks together.

Hal soon told his remarkable story: He had walked the Appalachian Trail, starting in Georgia and winding north more than 2,000 miles to Maine, in 2011.

"I didn't have dorm rooms and bars on the AT. I carried camping and cooking gear too."

"How long did it take?" Sue asked.

"Five months-plus. I set up supply drops at several spots along the trail."

Clement shook his head in disbelief and sipped his beer. "This is my first long trek; maybe the Appalachian will be next." He flashed a smile like he was joking. His Irish accent made me think of Mom.

I still was unsure I could do a measly 500 miles in Spain, even with running water and toilets, modern conveniences absent on the Appalachian Trail. I was impressed that Hal, at about my age, had the strength and courage to pull off 2,000 miles of roughing it.

Clement and Hal excused themselves and climbed the stairs to clean up before dinner. Many more trekkers would hear Hal's Appalachian Trail stories during the next month.

Sue and I moved to the seats next to the wall so we could view the comings and goings at the reception counter.

"What do you think of the wine?" I asked Sue.

"It's good, real smooth." We drank chardonnay at home, but we would become fond of the Tempranillo in eastern Spain.

Three trekkers grabbed the last beds in the albergue. I recognized one, who was limping, as the guy we saw atop the mountain pass, suffering from a knee injury. On his slow climb to the dorm, he used a trekking pole like a cane and moaned in pain. I knew there was no way he had descended the mountain without considerable help.

The clock behind the bar showed it was 5:30, nearly dinner time. I was famished and wondered if I would like pilgrim food. I was not too picky an eater as long as my taste buds didn't contact bell peppers or cilantro. A few minutes later a couple came down the stairs, ordered drinks at the bar, and, as they turned around, I offered, "You're welcome to sit here."

As they sat opposite us, I thought they could be brother and sister. I sensed they were experienced trekkers, considering their worn hiking boots and clothes as well as the confidence they brought to our table. Gitta looked me in the eye as she introduced herself.

"How was your day on the Camino?" James stroked his gray beard.

"It was our first day," Sue began. "The mud and rocks over the mountain were tough, but the people have been so friendly."

"That's the Camino. The people, I mean. The trail will get better."

Have they done this before? I was about to ask when the young woman who checked us into the albergue waved us into the dining room.

The large, bright room at the back of the building featured several tables for two next to windows. As Sue and I sat at a small table, Gitta and James entered, scanned the room, and Gitta announced, "Let's all sit together!" She and James brought a table toward ours as the rest of us arranged tables in a line for 12. The server, who was not bothered by our forwardness, helped replace tablecloths and chairs.

Sue and I sat at one end and Gitta and James took chairs across from us. As we settled in, Clement, the young Irishman, nodded to Sue and me as he took the seat next to Gitta. I would never have considered rearranging the room, and I assumed Gitta was being pushy, but I later figured out that her act was quintessential Camino. For several of us at the table, it was also a fateful move that would lead us to share many joys and pains.

My eyes traveled around the table, and I realized that the people were not at all what I had expected at a communal pilgrim meal. No one looked capable of climbing Mount Everest. There were a dozen of us, aged 20s through 60s. Just ordinary folks. I was nervous as the server used Sue's camera to snap a group photo. Everyone seemed a bit on edge, but when the server placed bottles of Tempranillo on the table, a guy at the other end shouted, "Boy, do we need that!" We all laughed, and the pouring began. No one suggested we hold hands and bless the wine nor the meal. My fears about group prayer and touchy-feely gatherings were unfounded, at least for the moment.

James and I poured wine for the four of us, and I raised my glass, "Cheers, buen Camino!" We clinked glasses, and my curiosity about James and Gitta resurfaced. I didn't ask if they were a couple or brother and sister—not yet.

"So, it sounds like you have been here before."

"Yes, we both have," Gitta said. "I did the Camino for my 60th birthday."

I assumed that had to have been recently.

"Where did you start?"

I expected her to say, "St. Jean."

"Copenhagen, Denmark. That's where I live."

I checked my mental map of Europe. Roughly, I figured her trek had covered more than 2,000 miles.

"How long were you walking?"

"Six months."

It seemed unbelievable, but I did not doubt her veracity. I reckoned she could transport her wiry frame around the world.

Our server returned to take our orders for dinner as I digested Gitta's mind-boggling trek. The first course was a choice of mixed salad (topped with tuna fish), pasta marinara, or soup. The main course was pork chop, chicken or fish with potatoes. Desserts were flan, ice cream or fruit. The menu became familiar over the coming weeks. Sue would soon start calling the main course "pounded meat," and it usually came with a huge mound of French fries. We would tire of the main course until we learned we could have two starters instead (salad and pasta). The flan was our favorite dessert, especially when it came with caramel on top.

After we ordered, I asked, "So, James, you have done the Camino too?"

"Oh, sure, I started on skis in Siberia!"

Actually, he said, "Yes, after my first wife died, my best friend Bent and I hiked part of the Camino. It was his idea to honor my wife. That's how I met Gitta. Bent and I went to a Camino meeting in Copenhagen. Gitta was there too." That took care of my sibling question. There was an easy, conversational tone to James' voice.

After dinner, as I climbed the stairs to our dorm, I reviewed my day. First, the trail was not easy. I did not expect so much city walking, nor the mud and rocks. Second, the Camino was a community filled with cordiality, and the people so far were not judgmental. Even young people made me feel like they wanted to get to know me; I felt accepted. Third, the pilgrim meal was not great food, but the camaraderie around the table more than made up for it. Finally, so far, our first albergue had given me little to ruminate about. More lessons awaited.

But there was something else from my first day. Someone had shouted, "Come on in" when we paused at the entrance to the albergue.

The three words triggered my time machine that transported me to a winter day in sixth grade. It was raining when I returned home after school. I wiggled the door handle to our trailer. Locked.

"Dad, are you there?"

"Leave me alone."

"Dad?"

Soaking wet and cold, I stared at the door in disbelief. My eyes filled with tears as rain dripped from my chin. I remembered standing there for what seemed like forever. It has been one of my most stirring childhood memories. I never understood why he didn't let me in.

In the dorm, the man with the injured knee had taken the bed below Alejandro. We exchanged greetings as I lifted my toiletry bag and my nightclothes from my pack.

The toilet room was occupied. Within seconds, there were three of us at the sink in the men's room, brushing our teeth, and I unexpectedly felt at ease. In the toilet room, I changed into the athletic shorts and t-shirt I had brought for nighttime. I had been wearing my Teva sandals since we first arrived at the dorm. I saw a few men in just their underwear, a common sight on the Camino, but it was more unusual to see women in just underwear.

Sue was settling into her sleeping bag when I unrolled mine and tucked the liner inside. Our packs leaned against the wall under the window, next to our shoes.

"Good night, honey." I stood on my toes to kiss Sue.

I crawled into my liner and sleeping bag and propped my head against my tiny camping pillow. Across the crowded room, other trekkers prepared for bed. It was warm, so I unzipped my sleeping bag.

While people moved back and forth to the bathrooms, I recalled a year of nights in my family's 16-foot trailer. I slept shoulder-to-shoulder next to my brother Joe on the convertible dinette at the front while our parents squeezed into the mini-double bed at the back. For my middle-of-the-night toilet needs, the trailer park restrooms were a football field away. Many would find it hard to believe that the tiny trailer made me feel like I was home.

The crowded dorm room was my home for the night. I wished Sue were next to me, not on the bunk above. At about 10 o'clock, someone turned off the lights.

"Good night, everyone." A man's soothing voice—it sounded like James—emerged from the dark.

As I tried to get comfortable, the guy in the bed across from me chatted with a young Spanish woman who had a bunk near his. Actually, they were not exactly chatting. His knee must have felt better. I had heard bed-sharing was rare, but could happen in the dorm rooms. Luckily, this was not to be the night as they settled into their own beds.

During the next couple of hours, I heard people snorting (or were they farting?), snoring, breathing, turning over as bunk beds squeaked with every movement. The first day on the Camino had been memorable, so why was my brain suddenly racing? It must have been midnight when I jammed squishy blue plugs into my ears, but they barely muffled the concert. I briefly dismissed my tossing and turning as a result of jet lag, but I knew otherwise. My monkey mind had reappeared in the dark, and I worried that I would never be able to relax and sleep in such close quarters with people I hardly knew.

I finally got out of bed, snatched my sleeping liner and pillow, and felt my way in the dark to the common room, where I curled up on a short, plastic couch. Sleep came in spurts, and the night seemed to last forever.

8

Spittle, You're Next

I was jolted from my brief sleep. Lights flashed on, toilets flushed, showers ran, sleeping bags zipped, plastic rustled.

I poked my iPad; it was 7 a.m. A few trekkers talked at full volume as they loaded their backpacks. A woman two bunks away struggled with her balance as she pulled on cargo hiking shorts, then stretched a red, v-necked t-shirt over her head.

I had returned to the dorm and crawled into my sleeping bag about an hour earlier. I felt like I was 13 again, and Mom was about to start pestering me about being late for school if I didn't get up right away.

As I indulged my exhaustion, Sue's head appeared upside down over the edge of the bunk above me.

"Are you awake, honey?"

"Sort of."

"Did you sleep okay?" She was gauging my mood.

"Not really. You?"

"Better than in Pamplona."

I glimpsed one young hiker as he left the room carrying his backpack.

"We should probably get going," Sue suggested. "Checkout time is 8."

"I am not sure I can handle five weeks of this." I yanked everything out of my pack's main compartment and grabbed clothes for a quick change in the toilet room. I returned to my bunk, where the Ziplocs containing the rest of my clothes and toiletries were scattered at one end of my bed. The clothes bags would need compacting so I could get everything back into my pack, but first I picked up a small bag.

My sour mood showed. "My sleeping bag has to fit in *this*?"

After several attempts to roll up my sleeping bag so it would fit, I was flustered. I could feel the eyes behind me watching the rookie trekker from America, the old man who couldn't figure out how to pack. I glanced across at Alejandro, who was finishing his packing. I was certain he had witnessed my failed efforts.

My heartbeat and breathing quickened as I struggled to control my descent. I was consumed by self-consciousness, but my brain was just getting started as it yanked me back to my freshman year at Oxnard High School in Southern California. The memory came from one of my darkest closets, one that I had kept locked for years. Why was it haunting me now? I was 14 years old and sat in the bleachers in the school gymnasium, looking up at the thick rope that hung from the rafters.

"Spittle, you're next," the coach barked, holding a clipboard that charted our PE class fitness test results.

Three-year-old Tarzan had more upper-body strength than I had in high school, so I was certain my arms could not propel me high enough to touch the knot high above. I stepped toward the rope as my classmates' whispers and snickers followed. I stared at the knot for what seemed like an eternity before uttering five words that I would hear repeated mockingly in the school hallways for days: "Coach, I can't do it."

"But you have to try, Spittle. C'mon!"

"Please don't cry," I told myself as my legs wobbled under the pressure. The boys before me had followed the coach's instructions to jump, grab the rope, and use their feet on the rope to stabilize themselves as they worked their way up. In sixth grade, I couldn't even make it halfway across the monkey bars. Three years later, I did the only thing I knew how to do. I turned and walked back to the bleachers and sat, avoiding eye contact with other kids. I felt beyond humiliated, but somehow I did not break down. Another feeling swelled inside me as I clenched my teeth and fists while I breathed through my nose so deeply that I was sure the other boys noticed. My eyes focused on the hardwood floor. I was pissed off—at the coach, at my classmates, at myself. If I could have canned the energy from my anger, I would have squeezed the can open, drained its contents into my mouth, and climbed the goddamn rope like Popeye. Then I would have told my pot-bellied coach, "Now, Bluto, you climb the stupid rope!"

Kneeling on my bed, I looked again at the sleeping bag and the small sack in my hands. I was determined not to wimp out as I had done with the rope climb. The anger from ninth grade felt fresh as I grabbed the sleeping bag and, with my tightly clenched fist, punched it into the sack. I glanced behind me to see the reactions, but I was startled to see that no one was watching. In fact, most people had left. Three-year-old Tarzan was likely more mature than I was on my second morning on the Camino de Santiago. And no one witnessed Popeye's sleeping-bag victory.

I tightened the drawstring on my sleeping bag's container and raised my hands to my forehead as my chin fell to my chest. After a minute, I crammed everything into my pack, buckled it shut, and shouted to my bunk mate above: "Ready, honey?"

It was after 8 a.m. when we finally tied our shoelaces, lifted our packs onto our shoulders, and descended the stairs. We were the last ones out, by a long shot. And the morning was about to get worse.

"I'll feel better after coffee and breakfast," I reckoned as we reached the main drag through Uterga. However, if the village had breakfast, it hid it from us.

As we stepped silently toward coffee and food in Puente la Reina—at least two hours away—I added to my mental checklist of lessons: Get clothing bags packed the night before to save time in the morning. And, always keep a meal or two in my pack. I had brought packets of instant Starbucks coffee, but that didn't help at our first albergue because it didn't offer kitchen facilities.

Another lesson arrived gradually as my frustration waned. Even though my backpack felt less comfortable than it did on the first day, and my stomach grumbled, my senses feasted on the spectacular scenery in rural northern Spain. It was impossible to stay grumpy. A mile out of Uterga, spring growth created a lush tunnel beneath tall shrubs along a section of the trail. A cluster of oak trees framed a six-foot marble statue of a religious figure perched behind a bench. "Rest here, pilgrims," it seemed to offer. Birds joined nature's chorus. Blankets of mustard paved the ground under a budding olive grove. I had no idea Spain was so gorgeous. The trail that morning was easy, lacking the mud and rocks from our first day. My lesson sounded corny, but it was clear: The magic of the Camino was strong.

I was trying to remember what coffee smelled like when we finally found the Hotel Jakue bar at the entrance to Puente la Reina. We were caffeine-deprived and beyond hungry.

"Do you smell that?" I almost shouted as we entered the bar. The aroma of coffee was so enticing I could taste it.

"That looks so good!" Sue stared at the counter. A "*tortilla de patatas*" sign announced a frittata-like pie. We had to have some. We would come to know it as a Spanish omelette with eggs, potatoes, and sometimes cheese. Our backpacks slid to the floor as we stepped to the counter. "Hola. What can I get for you?" Her eyes twinkled with the knowledge that she was looking at two hungry, grateful customers.

We each ordered a piece of the pie, orange juice, and coffee. I almost ordered the whole pie. As I tasted the first bite, I closed my eyes. "I am always going to remember this breakfast!" After finishing, I ordered another round. That's when I saw the sign offering sandwiches to go.

Breakfast for two and lunch for the road came to €10 each. For at least one morning, the Hotel Jakue bar was Heaven on Earth. An adage had made its first appearance: The Camino will provide.

On our way out, I waved to the woman behind the counter as she arranged croissants on a tray, and I said, "*Tostada esta muy bien*!" I even rubbed my stomach.

She waved back. “Buen Camino!”

Outside, Sue looked up “*tostada*” in the Spanish dictionary on her phone. “You told her ‘toast is fine!’” We both laughed aloud as we turned past a 12th century church across the street. It was a welcome relief to hear myself laugh—at myself.

It was late morning and the sunny day was warming to the 70s. After a climb of several hundred feet, we found Alejandro, the young Spaniard who had the upper bunk across from us in Uterga. He sat on the edge of the trail, examining his bare feet, and looked at us with a pained expression.

“Are you all right?” Sue asked.

“I think I’m getting blisters.”

Sue removed her pack and knelt for feet inspection. Bright red spots the size of dimes marked the balls of his feet and one big toe.

“You need to put something on these spots. Do you have anything?”

Alejandro shook his head. He was no veteran trekker, that was for sure.

“We have blister pads. Do you want some?”

“Yes, please.”

Sue removed our first aid kit from her pack and passed Alejandro an alcohol pad so he could wipe the spots. She pealed the backing off several small, thin adhesive pads and handed them to Alejandro one at a time.

“Oh, that feels better!” He massaged his toes and soaked up the relief.

Alejandro was about the age of our three sons, and, as Sue helped him, I remembered times she had doctored scrapes on our boys. She rarely relished the role of nurse, but that never prevented her tender loving care. Alejandro had been an important part of my feeling welcome at our first albergue; I was pleased our up-and-down morning had delivered us to his side at just the right time.

“Thank you.” He gave Sue the grateful look a son gives his mom.

“Of course. You should be able to get more pads in a pharmacy.”

He squeezed into his sneakers as nurse Sue and I returned to day two of a journey that had already caused me to question my script.

Just a few minutes ahead, alongside a freshly plowed field, a green tractor towed a wheeled contraption unlike anything I had ever seen. Three men wore baseball-style caps and sat in seats, riding just above the ground at the back of the wide, towed vehicle. They pulled seedlings from flats on a shelf in front of them, reached down, and planted them as they inched along the rows. My gaze turned to the other side of the valley where a hillside was nearly covered with grazing sheep moving in a herd, followed by a sprinting black-and-white sheep dog. A strolling shepherd waved as we passed on the path, which was lined with yellow mustard and bright red poppies.

My walking meditation was interrupted by a sound coming from my left.

"Cuckoo."

We were passing a small farm dotted with shade trees in a shallow valley when we heard it again.

"Cuckoo."

Back home in California, the source of that sound hung on walls.

Sue and I wondered where the farmer hid the clock.

"I can't believe there is a clock outside on the farm," I reasoned. "But it sure sounds like one."

"Have you ever heard of cuckoo birds?"

"Yes, but are they real?" I was unsure. "I always presumed they were make-believe."

"I think they're real and, from the sounds, I think there are quite a few of them around here."

The cuckoo bird developed a life of its own on our Camino. We would joke with each other many times the rest of the way whenever we heard "Cuckoo." "There's that clock again!" Someone later told us when we heard the cuckoo bird, we must touch our wallets right away for good luck. We fell for it.

After a brief stop for a snack, we approached the village of Cirauqui, which featured a hilltop 13th century church. We turned a corner of a narrow cobblestone street and came face-to-face with the Danish couple who sat across from us at the albergue dinner the previous night.

"Hello Sue and Reg!" Gitta greeted us from a bench beside the trail.

"How has the trail been for you today?" James asked.

"You were right, wider and easier than our first day," I said.

"Let's walk together." Gitta started up a steep, winding, cobblestone street between restored stone-walled, two-story buildings.

"Sue, your poles are too long," Gitta said. "Let me show you."

James and I continued as Sue dropped back for an extensive lesson about the proper use of trekking poles. James was a cultural anthropologist, but was at ease talking politics after I told him I taught American government. I got the impression he was an avid *New York Times* and *Atlantic Monthly* reader. My students would have enjoyed him as a guest lecturer.

"I used to live in New York City," he shared at one point.

Sue tried Gitta's ideas, but eventually developed her own style. Gitta was a coach to her core. She had trekked from Copenhagen to Santiago and probably knew what she was talking about, so I asked her for a few pointers when she finished with Sue. It would be several days before I learned to allow the poles to swing back on forth with a gentle tap on the ground rather than my more heavy-handed poke Gitta said could eventually cause shoulder, elbow and wrist problems.

"You don't need to swing your arms so much," she taught. Gitta's instruction would be too intense for some, but I soaked up her attention and saw Gitta as a role model who could save me from embarrassing mistakes. It reminded me of other times when I was the new guy trying to find my way. For the second time in one day, I retrieved events from my freshman year in high school.

My parents, Joe and I had moved out of the 50-by-8 trailer and into a small apartment next to Oxnard's St. John's Hospital, where Mom was a housekeeper. The apartment building was modest, but luxurious compared to the trailer park. I welcomed the move, except for one byproduct: I was once again a new kid as I began high school. On the first day, in the huge cafeteria, I sat at the empty end of a long table next to a wall. I opened my sack lunch and, as was my habit, kept my eyes on my food to avoid seeing what I imagined were stares.

"Could I sit here?"

I looked up at the older boy who held a tray and awaited my answer.

"Sure, er, have a seat."

I bit into my bologna sandwich.

"I'm Jake. You're new to Oxnard High, aren't you?"

"Yeah." I nervously searched for more words. He asked where I had gone to junior high and if I had ever participated in athletics. He nodded and smiled at my answers.

"You should go out for a sport, Reg. It's a great way to meet people."

"I'm terrible at sports, believe me." I was letting down my guard and soaking up the relief that came with a feeling I rarely found: trust.

"You should try cross-country. All you have to do is run. No ball to catch or throw. You're thin, which is good for running." Jake was slightly shorter than me, probably five-nine, and slim, but much more muscular than I was.

"I'm not exactly fast."

"Come to our first practice today. We need more guys for the freshman team."

I avoided the promise Jake sought, but told him I would think about it. After school, I closed my locker and turned toward home when I felt a hand on my back.

"Hey, Reg, practice is this way."

Jake called me his friend when he introduced me to the team and the coach. During a one-mile run on the first practice day, I was running out of gas at the end of my third lap around the track.

"You're doing fine, Reg. It will get easier."

Jake had lapped me and slowed to run my last lap at my side, even though he had already finished the mile.

It turned out he was the star of the team. I stayed with cross-country for the season and earned a locker in the screened-off athletes' section of the locker room. I was the slowest runner, but the star had brought me to the team, so that part of my high school day was without the ridicule that often followed me in the hallways. Jake couldn't protect me from the rope climb, but he guided me to a refuge for a slice of my freshman year. He had offered me a chance to try something far outside my comfort zone, and he was there to support my effort every lap of the way.

I have often wondered why I embraced Jake's outreach, but have rejected so many others for decades since high school. Cross-country exposed me as a terrible runner, but his compassion gave me the security I longed for.

Gitta did not have Jake's low-key approach, but I sensed sincerity. I told myself to accept her offer and resist my natural inclination to go it alone. As I had done with Jake, I seized the opportunity to learn from Gitta's trekking experience.

After we left the hilltop village of Cirauqui, the trail followed an ancient road and took us over the sturdy remains of a stone-arched bridge built by the Romans. Gitta and I waded through tall grass and weeds to photograph the side of the bridge. I wondered if the new bridges spanning the nearby A-12 highway would be around in a couple thousand years.

Sue and I pushed on as Gitta and James paused for a break. We crossed an impressive arched medieval bridge over the Rio Saldo, one of many such spans, and decided to hunt for beds in the tiny, but cute village of Lorca. We had come 12 miles for a total of 21 since leaving Pamplona in our westward journey across Spain, well short of our plan to average 15 miles a day.

An arched entrance led us into the restored, stone-walled La Bodega del Camino, a private albergue offering a small bar. We were the first to arrive for the day, and Sue didn't protest my request for a small private room next to a dorm room and a shared bathroom. Our host dated another passport stamp, which featured an archway mirroring the albergue's entrance with a scallop shell and trekking stick inside.

The stamps are used by the Pilgrim Office in Santiago when trekkers apply for their Camino completion certificates, or compostelas. Trekkers who want one of the certificates must walk at least the last

100 kilometers (about 62 miles) of the Camino while getting two stamps a day in their passport from albergues, bars, or other places. Pilgrims are expected to show at least one stamp a day from other parts to establish their starting point, although the stamps before the last 100 kilometers are not required for the compostela. I hoped a framed compostela would hang on a wall at home after we returned.

As the innkeeper showed us to our upstairs room, she asked, "Would you like an evening meal and breakfast in the morning?" We heartedly accepted both, especially breakfast—anything to avoid another morning without fuel. Our room, just €25 for the two of us, was big enough for a double bed and small end tables with lamps. Sue celebrated that our bed was made up with sheets, pillows, a blanket and bedspread. The bunks, which cost €8 each, in the adjoining dorm had only a folded blanket at the end of the bed.

"This room is a great deal," she said. "It's only €9 more than two bunk beds. And I won't have to worry about repacking my sleeping bag."

We emptied our backpacks and placed the Ziploc bags and other gear on our bed. As Sue took a photograph of our gear for our blog, we heard the voices of Gitta and James, who were settling into beds in the dorm. We said hello before we returned to organize our packs for a less frustrating exit in the morning.

During my afternoon shower, I luxuriated as the hot water soothed my shoulders and back while I anticipated a hot meal in the downstairs bar with Gitta and James.

The four of us were the only diners in the downstairs bar. The proprietor who checked us in earlier performed double duty as the server, and when she brought the first course, Gitta urged us to eat everything on our plates. "You will need every ounce of energy." She gave me a disapproving look when I scooted the tuna atop my salad to the side of my plate. I recalled times when my mom looked at the fried beef liver on my plate. "Eat your liver, Reg. People in China are starving." As a child, I knew better than to say anything. I figured that was best at the Camino table as well, so I ate my tuna.

After dinner, as we exited the bar, about half a dozen noisy American bicyclists were checking in for the night. I asked one cyclist who wore black Lycra shorts how his ride was going.

"Well, it was rocky coming down the mountain today, but we did more than 60 miles from St. Jean. We had to carry our bikes part of the way."

"How far are you going?"

"All the way to Santiago!"

On our way upstairs, I asked James if bicyclists could earn a compostela.

"Sure. They have to do at least the last 200 kilometers (124 miles) rather than just 100."

I stretched out between the fresh sheets next to my wife in our quiet room. My second day had been an emotional roller coaster of events that had jarred my memory bank. I closed my eyes and breathed slowly, deeply. In my wildest dreams, I would never be as strong as Popeye, but I hungered to mimic his belief in himself.

BODEGAS IRACHE
BODEGAS IRACHE
VINO

9

I Broke My Leg

In just two days, yellow markers had guided us through a feast of experiences and sights that defied predictability. The third day held answers to a series of mysteries.

Was that a volcano or a castle? How can we possibly go that far? Why is the water red? How can she walk on a broken leg? Why would second coffee become a ritual?

The day had started with the introduction of a breakfast staple in Spanish bars: fresh, thick bread that exited a conveyor-belt toaster crispy brown on the outside and squishy inside. I could have eaten it all morning, especially after I smothered it with butter and homemade jam. Coffee and orange juice completed the trio that would greet us most mornings.

"That room was great," I told Sue as we finished our first albergue breakfast.

"Yeah, but we can't expect that every night." Sue was hoping I was developing a thicker skin for what was ahead.

I reflected on the many people we met in just two days, but especially James and Gitta, who had taken us under their wings. I assumed they enjoyed passing their knowledge to two trekkers who knew diddly-squat about the Camino. And we would not be the only ones who would benefit from their compassion over the next two weeks.

After breakfast, our priority was food for lunch and emergencies. This time, luck was on our side at a supermarket on the uphill road leading from our albergue in Lorca. In the tiny market, we found fresh bread, cheese, bananas, and a package of shelled, salted peanuts. Plus, a chocolate bar, which became our trailside indulgence.

A few miles later, we descended about 300 feet before crossing a medieval, arched stone bridge over the Rio Iranzu in Villatuerta. We had already taken note of a common sight in villages: bars, backpacks, and pilgrims, a combination that characterized Camino rest stops. We had been on our feet for two hours when Sue had an idea that would become a morning ritual.

"A second cup of coffee would be great, don't you think?"

A small bar conveniently popped up around the corner, and it came with a bonus: a familiar couple who sat outside. Ian and Marion had dined at the other end of the narrow table at our first albergue in Uterga. Oxford, England was their home. They invited us to join them after we ordered coffees inside.

"How far are you going today?"

Ian considered my question. "Hopefully, the town on Mount Castillo. You could see it from the trail a bit ago."

Sue shook her head. "We saw a mountain shaped like a pointed volcano, but Reg and I can't possibly make it that far today."

"Actually, there is a castle at the top, and even you Americans can get that far this afternoon." His left elbow nudged my arm as he grinned.

"Look at this." Ian opened the guidebook to a map, which showed Mount Castillo was nine miles away.

"You will walk much farther than you think you can. Places that seem so far away come up much more quickly than you expect."

I pictured Ian leading an African safari, and I already knew that I would like to join his tour. I was near certain that he and Marion, who were about our age, had many years of adventurous travel behind them. Marion at first declined being in a group photo that Sue wanted to take, saying she hated being in pictures. Later, she gave the go-ahead when Sue asked again.

After our break, we traveled with them for a short spell, then, as would become the norm, we were separated by different paces. Our paths were destined to cross many more times in the days ahead, including the restorative rest stops for second coffees.

On the warm, sun-filled late morning, we skirted the city of Estella, crossed the N-111 highway, and passed a vineyard of gnarled grapevine stumps. I imagined the hills would be brown, and the trail more crowded in the heat of summer. We were low on water, so the timing was perfect as we approached an iconic pilgrimage site: Bodegas Irache, a rest stop like no other. I passed the benches to a sturdy rock wall with two spigots. I twisted the one on the right and filled my first water bottle. I pulled out my second plastic bottle and slowly turned the left tap. This time, I sipped from the bottle. I heard children giggling behind me and whirled around to see a boy and girl, with wonder on their faces.

"*Agua roja!*" (Red water) I exclaimed, holding the bottle aloft.

"No, it's wine," said the boy, probably kindergarten age, in a Spanish accent. Their parents joined me and their children in laughter.

The wine came courtesy of the adjacent winery. It was mouth-puckering bitter. Beyond the rest area was a Benedictine monastery with a stone tower, where monks had served from the tenth century until 1985. Oak-covered mountains provided the backdrop.

Minutes later, Sue and I sat on a bench at the rest stop eating hunks of bread and cheese when Lena limped toward us, with pain written on her face. We had met her on the trail during our second day as she accompanied a group of trekkers about her age, early twenties. This time she was alone.

Sue reverted to Mom mode. "What's wrong, Lena?"

"I broke my leg!"

Sue and I looked at each other.

"How can you even walk?" Sue asked.

Lena, who was from Poland, sat at the end of the bench and removed her boots as if each tug brought discomfort. She was the only pilgrim we had seen who wore a skirt. She flipped her long brown hair over her shoulder and leaned back into the bench, closing her eyes and exhaling audibly.

Lena pointed to the elastic wrap on her right knee. "This helps a lot." As we finished our lunch, she rewrapped her knee and refilled her water bottle. Like us, she could not resist sips of red wine, and she smiled at us after her tasting.

Sue was concerned. "Are you going to be all right?"

"I will be fine. Thank you."

As we returned to the trail we dismissed Lena's "broken-leg" comment as a lost-in-translation moment. Lena was the third young trekker we had known who was struggling with injuries. We both complained about our aches, but managed to work through the discomfort. I wondered if our luck would continue.

So far, with the exception of the mountain out of Pamplona, the path had been a wide, mostly dirt track crisscrossing the N-111 highway through green rolling hills. Our shoes overheated on sun-baked sections of asphalt. With every passing hour, Mount Castillo zoomed closer. Soon, we could make out the ruins of St. Stephens Castle on the mountaintop. By mid-afternoon, we reached our home for the night, Villamayor de Monjardín, built two-thirds of the way up the mountain, high enough for views of the green countryside.

Sue pointed to the trail far behind us. "So Ian was right; we have made it to the castle mountain in one day. Look how far we have come."

I looked across the vast expanse to the mountain behind our morning coffee bar stop. "That's unbelievable. Maybe we *can* walk across Spain!"

"Should we hike up to the castle?"

Our tired bodies answered my question.

A new private albergue that was not in the guidebook caught our interest, so we opened the front door and peered inside. Private hostels were more expensive and nicer than most municipal albergues. This one, run by two men in their twenties, would set a standard for us. It was in a restored building, and the inside was contemporary and clean. We were among the first to arrive for the day. We found our newly renovated room at the top of the stairs. It was tiny and pillow cases, sheets, and blankets were stacked at the end of the bunk beds, along with pillows. My gaze drifted out the window to the church tower and trekkers on the street below.

I looked in a door at the end of our room. "Come see this!"

Our private room included a modern, fully outfitted bathroom with a large shower. I was thrilled, but a pang of guilt accompanied such luxury on a pilgrimage. Another part of me spoke louder: "Enjoy it while you can."

The wide stone staircase outside our albergue led to a Dutch Christian hostel, which featured a bar with outdoor seating in a small plaza. We signed up for the pilgrim meal and carried our drinks outside in the still-warm late afternoon.

I savored my first sip of my pint of Spanish lager. "I wonder who will join us for dinner tonight." The beer was barely better than Budweiser, but it was cold and refreshing. Four empty plastic chairs around us were soon filled as first Gitta and James arrived, followed by Ian and Marion. All were staying in a dorm room in our albergue. I was honored that they chose to sit at our table.

Ian was the first to speak. "Nice albergue, but only one private room, and it was already taken."

I looked at Sue.

Ian nodded. "I figured it was you." As I listened to him weave a travel story, I sipped my beer and mused about what it would be like to have him in my poker group back in California. Anything to distract me from my lousy card skills, another imperfection I worried about enough that I sometimes stayed away from the monthly games. Ian met people with ease. He was relaxed, yet purposeful, and people wanted to listen to him. And he enjoyed the spotlight.

As the first course was served after we had moved indoors, our table became even more international. Isabelle, a Brazilian whose outspoken nature and charisma would add pizzazz to our next few days, joined our group. She drew the ire of pilgrims in the dorm later by loudly (she seemed to have just one volume) Skyping with her boyfriend from Brazil. The call was after quiet time (10 p.m.), and she angled her laptop at one point so her boyfriend could see everyone else in the room. So much for privacy.

"Hi Clement!" Someone shouted from the table.

We had enjoyed getting to know the young Irishman during happy hour and dinner at our first albergue. He stopped to say hello, but told us he couldn't stay. He had descended the trail from the mountaintop and said he was going on to the next village.

"The castle's great; you should go up!"

As Clement turned and trudged away, I sensed he was searching for something. A girlfriend? Himself? Or just a good time? I was sad I might not see him again as he leaped ahead.

I wondered where my Camino would lead me. My worries from three days before had been replaced by my new sense of comfort that steered away from my usual labyrinth of anguish. But I remained aware of the nagging insecurity that always loomed like a cloud. For the moment, my mind remained refreshingly clear.

10

One Large Bathroom for All

Back in California, I had dwelled on a slew of questions as I anticipated the Camino de Santiago.

How far will I travel each day? How many days will it take? What will it cost? Can I walk all the way to Santiago? Will I be comfortable in the albergues?

Three days and 33 miles into my journey, it had veered in unforeseen directions. At the beginning of my fourth day, I was learning to celebrate the surprises, but a new worry threatened to derail the adventure for me—and Sue.

The early morning sun cast its rays on Mount Castillo's peak, and the castle ruins glowed. I turned around to photograph the castle before it disappeared behind us. We started early after a lousy breakfast at the new albergue featuring packaged pastries, sugary juice, and weak coffee. I was tempted to open the instant Starbucks in my pack, but pondered if it would be rude to make my own coffee. Besides, we would likely stop at a bar along the way for our second coffee. I remembered just two days before we had to wait hours for breakfast, so I tried to be grateful for fuel to start the day.

New albergues like the one we had just departed appeared in response to the Camino's fast-growing popularity. A record 272,412 compostelas were issued in 2010, the year the movie *The Way* was released. Many credited (or blamed) the movie, at least partially, but

2010 was also a Holy Year, when it is said that pilgrims reaching Santiago are absolved of all their sins.

In medieval times, the Camino started at a walker's front door. When trekkers finally reached Santiago, it symbolized a new beginning. They stripped off all clothing, which was burned in a caldron. Vendors waited with new clothes. Some continued several more days to Finisterre, on the Atlantic coast, known as the End of the World. Other caminos have gained popularity in recent years, including the Camino del Norte along Spain's north coast and the path through Portugal. Both end in Santiago.

The morning air on our fourth day was cool, so we wore our thin down jackets. As usual, we started the day with shoulders, calves, and thighs that were ready to stage a mutiny. As the day warmed, we stopped for a break and removed our shoes to let our feet catch their breath.

Sue grimaced as she removed her left shoe and sock. "Uh-oh, come see this, honey."

She pried apart the smallest two toes. They were bright red where they had been rubbing against each other. Her small toes nested under the toes next to them, causing friction and the early sign of potentially debilitating blisters.

Later, we played leapfrog and shared casual conversations with a Dutch man who gripped a tall walking stick and carried a daypack on his broad shoulders. His companion was a rambunctious, small, short-haired black-and-white dog. An hour after we had last passed the pair, we rounded a corner where a sturdy-sized woman was standing, looking anxiously down the path.

"Hello, are you all right?" Sue asked.

"Did you see a man with a dog?"

"We just passed them a couple of miles back. They should be here soon."

"Oh, thank you. I parked our caravan (travel trailer) near here."

No dorm room for the "Caravan Man," as we called him. There were many ways to do the Camino.

Our day ended after 12 miles in Torres del Rio next to the Rio Linares. The small village featured a striking, 12th-century, stone octagonal church linked to the Knights Templar. The knights were sent by the pope to protect pilgrims during medieval days. We did not see any armored knights on horseback during our entire trek, nor did we feel we needed protection, but we passed walled stone castles and churches that recalled a different time.

Cities and villages on the Camino were built around Catholic churches, whose bells (whether recorded or authentic) often rang when we passed. Church towers were home to huge stork nests. Religion has attracted people to the Camino since the ninth century and most churches have continued to offer nightly pilgrim masses. Many have walked to honor the memory of St. James, Spain's patron saint, whose body is believed to be buried beneath the cathedral in Santiago.

We climbed the winding narrow street through Torres del Rio and peeked into the courtyard of the second of three albergues, La Pata & Oca. Tables and chairs outside a bar lured us inside to a small swimming pool and a bar that offered a pilgrim dinner and breakfast. The promise of food was the draw, so we registered and climbed one flight of stairs to a room with two sets of bunk beds; Gitta and James arrived later and took the other.

A discovery startled me. On our way to our bedroom, I opened an unmarked door leading to what I had dreaded for months: one large bathroom for all. My nightmares had featured a dressing room with benches next to a room with shower nozzles lined up along a tiled wall. But that scene turned out to be left over from my school days. I started breathing again when I saw the individual showers with doors. There were toilet stalls, also with doors.

As I washed off the day's grunge, I realized that the only thing albergue bathrooms exposed was my needless torment. Later, when I used a toilet while a woman sat in the next stall, my discomfort was as absent as gender signs on the bathroom door. But the woman did find out what my pee splash sounded like. Once again, I had obsessed over a ridiculous scenario created in darkness. I vowed to leave Eddie and his snapping towel where they belonged.

While Sue took her shower, I ventured downstairs for a beer—and two more Camino lessons.

The bartender presented me with a frothy pint of lager and said the charge was €4.50, almost six dollars and about 50 percent more than I had been paying. I dug into my pocket for more cash after I decided against challenging the price.

Outside, in the courtyard, there was Isabelle, the Brazilian Skyper, halfway through her beer. She waved and invited me to join her at a large round table in the late afternoon sun. I was happy to see Isabelle and was learning another lesson: When you least expected it, a trekker you thought you would not see again showed up and became a friend.

"Ah, beer," I sighed as I sat down. "But it was expensive."

"How much, Reg?"

"Four-fifty."

"Mine was three euro!" She took a big gulp. "Yummm. And it's probably better than yours!"

"How could that be?"

"Because they know you are a rich American!"

I giggled like a kid at Isabelle's remark. Still laughing, she held up her cheap beer as I snapped her picture. After finishing the first pint, this cheap American gave Isabelle €3 so she could get my second beer. Another lesson of the afternoon: Being American can be a liability.

We shared a tasty dinner with James, Gitta and Isabelle in a dim, basement-level dining room. Isabelle was impressed with Gitta's story about her trek from Copenhagen to Santiago several years before. And we learned James and Gitta were going home after Burgos, which was about one-third of the Camino.

I was alarmed by the news. "Why are you stopping?"

"We came to do the first part, since Bent and I did not do the whole thing. That will complete the Camino Bent and I started," James explained. He also said he and Gitta had already been on the trail for several weeks since beginning on the Le Puy route in France.

"And it rained almost every day in France," he lamented.

James and Gitta were my guideposts in their relaxed approach to walking and finding accommodations. They would be going home in about a week. I would miss talks with James about a wealth of topics, including insights from his experiences living in New York. We shared at least one characteristic: We would not be at home with a group of partying young pilgrims.

Seven days before, I had nervously waited in California for our trip to Spain. I yearned for a triumphant finish in Santiago after 500 miles, but wondered if I could carry my pack so far. I fretted about not being able to keep up with younger, stronger trekkers. I thought of fellow trekkers as competitors, not potential friends. I read blog posts about pilgrims who took buses to shorten their mileage, but I decided the trek would be a failure if I did not walk the entire route.

We had come 45 miles in four days, but my measurement of success had been transformed. I had already sacrificed the goal of completing the entire trek when weather moved us to begin in Pamplona instead of St. Jean, but I felt anything but a failure.

This was a journey to Santiago, but so far it was leading me to places not on a map. My feelings of inadequacy were replaced by a growing trust in the non-judgmental people I had met. Instead of retreating into my shell, I took time to get to know my fellow trekkers. The path was a culture of acceptance, and I felt quick-forming bonds with people. I sensed the transformative powers of the Camino, but I wondered if its wand would be a match for the ghosts that followed me.

On our fifth day Isabelle offered to reserve rooms for Sue and me, as well as Gitta, James, Ian and Marion, at a large, three-story albergue in downtown Logroño, a city of 145,000 on the Rio Ebro. She said her Portuguese fluency would be enough, and she was right.

Logroño, a university city, ended a guidebook stage. This was the first time we spent the night in a busy, end-of-stage place. Logroño's cobbled streets and medieval era buildings made it easy to imagine times hundreds of years before.

Sue and I found the old building housing our albergue and climbed two flights of wide stairs to a dark, narrow hallway and the check-in desk. We were delighted when we learned Isabelle had reserved an en suite room for us for just €35. As with many of our large accommodations, we wondered how we would get out if a fire broke out. In Logroño, there was only one stairway at the opposite end of the building. After we all checked into the albergue, our group gathered for alfresco drinks at a nearby bar.

Isabelle bid goodnight after dinner, and I thanked her again for booking our stay. As she exited the bar, Sue said what we all felt, "That was nice of her to book our rooms. But I am not sure she is really walking the Camino."

Isabelle was a mystery. We never saw her on the trail, but she appeared in the next town at a bar, where she bragged about her trekking speed. Sue rationalized the only steps Isabelle took were to the bus stops. We shared drinks and meals with her for several days. The women in our group didn't like her. To me, she was charming, but we did not see her after Logroño. Did she go home, or did she leap ahead? Those events, too, happened on the Camino.

Along with James, Gitta, Ian and Marion, we retired to the albergue common room. Gitta had offered to examine Marion's worsening blisters, and she opened her sewing/first aid kit as we all sat around the room and offered emotional support. Gitta methodically used a needle and thread to try to patch the bottom of Marion's feet. One blister was more than an inch round, and it was not a pretty sight. I couldn't bear to watch most of the time. We were all taken by Gitta's kindness and expertise that evening.

Marion disliked being the center of attention, but she was not afraid to speak out when she got comfortable. She occasionally let loose with funny zingers of her own. She and Ian came without sleeping bags and only one towel. They brought thin sleeping liners. In their defense, hostels in the UK, unlike those in Spain, generally have sheets, blankets and are heated. Some nights were cold in Spain, and there was usually only one blanket per bed.

Sue watched intently as Gitta finished work on Marion's feet. Sue's bandaging was preventing severe pain and blisters so far, but the redness and sensitivity were worrisome.

11

Party at the Underpass

If the Camino de Santiago had a complaint or suggestion box, I would have filled it on the morning of day six.

The bar across the street from our albergue was closed at 6:30 when we hoped to grab breakfast for an early start. We waited impatiently for an hour until the bar opened. The albergue's common room was mysteriously locked, so we couldn't even get hot water for instant Starbucks. At 7:30, trekkers could still not get into the locked kitchen.

My ankles and knees ached after the first hour of walking, thanks to cobblestones and concrete on the lengthy trek out of Logroño.

At the edge of the city, Sue spotted a large supermarket across a grassy area behind a fenced parking lot, but we explored the confusing perimeter for 10 minutes before we found a way into the store. It was just what we needed, extra steps. Then, the store required us to leave our backpacks at the door. Tom had his backpack stolen in the movie when he had to leave it outside a bar. We knew better than to leave valuables in our pack, but we still worried that our packs would be taken.

I reviewed my complaints: late breakfast, cobblestone path, extra steps, no backpacks.

Rationality eased my frustrations as I imagined the Camino's replies.

“This is Spain, not California! Our days start later to allow everyone to ease into the day. Chill!”

“You complain about medieval cobblestones? Really? Go walk your California freeways!”

“What did you expect? Did you think you could just call the supermarket with your order and have it delivered to you on the trail? Also, didn’t you consider the food that would be spilled when your pack knocked things off the shelves as you turned around?”

I realized my complaints were selfishly trivial. We had trekked 58 miles in five days, with almost 400 to go. Sure, there were hardships, plenty of them. But no one said the trek would be easy. If day six’s problems were worthy of complaints, then we would have quit on the spot had we known what awaited us.

A half hour after leaving the supermarket (with our unmolested backpacks), a long tunnel under the A-12 highway offered relief from the warm sun and another social opportunity, this one exclusively North American. I greeted a teen-ager in board shorts who sat against the tunnel wall next to his backpack.

“Where are you from, Mark?”

“Maine; I’m on spring break from high school.”

Two women joined our party, propping their backpacks and poles next to Mark’s. It was Huan and Linda, Canadians slightly beyond college age whom I recognized from the trail the past two days. It was like a bar stop without the plastic chairs and table.

Linda wiped her face on her sleeve. “It’s hot today. The shade and breeze feel fantastic.” She stood with her hands on her hips and was the only hiker in the group wearing long trousers.

“But at least there’s no humidity like we get in Toronto,” Huan said while she sat cross-legged on the concrete near Mark, who snacked from a plastic bag in his lap.

I was still processing the fact that an American high school kid was trekking on the Camino.

“Did you come to Spain by yourself?”

“I’m with a friend and her mom.” Mark paused to pop a few peanuts into his mouth, then continued.

"Three weeks ago, I was sitting in my math class when my friend told me she was going to walk part of the Camino with her mom. I said, 'I wish I could do that!' When I got home, I got a text from her. 'My mom says you should come with us!'"

"That's amazing, Mark," Huan said. "Where are they?"

"They're slow, so I went ahead. I'll wait later for them to catch up."

"How do you like the albergues?" Huan asked.

"They're super cheap, but my friend's mom almost clobbered a snoring guy in the next bunk last night."

There was a break in the conversation as the Canadians pulled snacks from their backpacks.

Mark was not finished with his enthusiasm. "My friends can't believe I'm doing this trek. The people are great. There is one thing I hate about it, though."

We all waited for him to explain.

"I have to go back to school soon and can't walk all the way to Santiago."

"You'll have to come back and finish your Camino," Linda suggested.

"I know; you're right."

He looked up at Linda. "How do you like the albergues?"

"We're on a tight budget, so they're perfect. A bunch of us cooked a huge pot of pasta in the kitchen last night. We made a salad, and the whole meal cost us €2 each!"

"I'd be up for that anytime!" Mark said.

I couldn't have agreed less. Shopping, cooking, and cleaning up sounded terrible after a full day of trekking. Was it my age or just laziness?

Another Canadian soon joined us. Quincy, old enough to be their father, knew Huan and Linda, and I assumed they had been traveling together. I admired his white Panama hat.

It was time to be party-poopers. Sue and I donned our backpacks and bid so long, knowing we would likely see Mark and the Canadians over the coming days.

Bargain hunters like Mark, Huan and Linda love the Camino. Those who stay in inexpensive hostels and cook in the kitchens, can probably travel on €25 a day, or less, depending on where they shop for food. Some trekkers live on the Camino, going back and forth many times. Gitta said she could spot them and insisted we give them money. The people she pointed out were mostly dirty and scruffy and sat on the street. I did not see people like that in the albergues.

A few hours after our party at the underpass, Sue and I stopped for an afternoon break in Navarette. Like many of the villages we had traveled through, it stood frozen in medieval times. A centuries-old church was the town's highest point, and narrow, cobbled streets dominated. A hunched-over woman pushed a bonnet-topped stroller through the plaza, where we sat on a bench. While we watched, she stopped many times as people fussed over her grandchild. I over-heard a young trekker remark, "That baby will be a teen-ager by the time they get to the end of town!"

It seemed like the Spanish people took time for each other, especially family and children. The pace of life in villages was slow, so different from California, where even free time was scheduled. Stores were places for conversation, not just restocking the pantry, and the locals didn't have to be pushing a grandchild to be stopped often to catch up with friends and relatives.

Hard-working people, mostly senior citizens, toiled on farms along the way. Modern machinery was often missing. Grains, wine grapes, and olive orchards connected each village. We learned many young people had left the farms (and even Spain) as unemployment soared in 2008 and several years afterward. As I passed through villages, I was greeted by "Hola" (Hello) or "*Buenos dias*" (Good morning) and always "*Buen Camino.*" (Happy trails) Old men and women waved from their front doors and balconies. On the rare occasion when we took a wrong turn, they pointed the right way and shouted, "Camino!" The pilgrimage has been part of their culture for centuries. No doubt, the Spanish people wanted us to feel at home.

Northeastern Spain was not flat. Other than the first day, we had not climbed mountains, but plenty of hills. Our sixth day was slightly hillier than usual, about 900 feet of elevation gain in the stage. As we climbed, Sue complained, "Martin Sheen never walked up a hill!"

The path often crossed highways through tunnels or over pedestrian bridges. Occasionally, we were forced to dash between cars as we crossed highways. Some stretches were all countryside, as we saw parts of Spain only hikers see.

Many of my fellow trekkers hiked for deeply religious or personal reasons. I saw it in their faces and occasionally heard it in their stories. There were people from all parts of the world; age differences spanned many decades. An engineer from Australia bunked next to a farmer from South Korea. A college dropout shared a meal seated alongside a college professor from Denmark. A grandmother from Croatia paused next to the trail to help a strapping young Brazilian treat his blisters.

Increasing numbers have come to Spain for the tradition, the beauty, the challenge, or to claim they conquered the Camino de Santiago. But it offered so much more. As my fellow walkers and I shared dinners, dorm rooms, bathrooms, inconveniences, and the trail, the Camino reached beyond everyday life to touch us in unique ways. It happened to me, but I couldn't explain how it worked, so I called it magic.

We ended our sixth day after 12 miles. My shoulders had hurt most of the day, and I experimented with various strap adjustments, but nothing eased the soreness. Our guidebook showed that instead of extending six miles to the next town, we could detour slightly to the tiny (150 people) village of Ventosa, with just one albergue. Of course, it was uphill. At the San Saturnino, we entered through a bead curtain, which helped keep flies away. A surly manager with a strong German accent checked us in and stamped our passports with a drawing of the village church and scallop shell. I was disappointed that no meals were offered. I climbed the stairs to our narrow dorm room, lined with five sets of bunks and one small window.

Four trekkers who appeared to be typical college age sat on their bunks and ignored my "Hola!" (so un-Camino-like) as I brushed past them toward a vacant lower bunk, leaving the top one for Sue. There were times I got tired of all the greetings everywhere, but the lack of at least a "*Buenos dias*" felt like a snub.

It was common for trekkers, no matter the nationality, to say basic greetings in Spanish. After that, English was most common, unless there was a group of a particular nationality. I usually began with the native language, thinking it showed respect. From the reactions I got, I suspected the locals would rather not listen to my awful pronunciation and word choices, so they switched to English quickly. Sometimes they laughed, like in Paris when I asked for a fork in French, followed by "*por favor*." (Please, but in Spanish.) On the Camino, one inn manager asked how to spell my last name and had trouble understanding my English alphabet over the phone. Sue saved the day, taking the phone to spell our name in Spanish. I suppose I could have just said, "*saliva*," Spanish for spittle.

We expected more than a two-hour journey to the next village in the morning, so we needed breakfast and lunch food. We saw no market in Ventosa, but had noticed a closet-sized store in the albergue downstairs, so we dumped our packs on our beds and retraced our steps. We bought crackers, cheese, fruit, another chocolate bar, and some yogurt, which we stored in the communal fridge for breakfast. Like many hostels, there was a kitchen with a stove, sink, pots, pans and dishes.

And a laundry! I found it through the back door, across a small courtyard, in a tiny building. I loaded our clothes into a washer as I greeted two American women, Hannah and Emily. Later, Sue opened the washer to hang our clothes on the clothesline when Hannah pitched a fit. As Sue emptied the washer, the out-going Hannah interrupted, "But that's the American's laundry," moving to block Sue from getting to the washer.

"I'm the American's wife!" Sue told me later than she thought Hannah was going to grab her and pull her away from the washing machine.

After a late-afternoon shower, I returned to our bunk and Emily, Hannah's travel partner, was asleep in the bed across from mine, with her back turned toward me. Emily had not been friendly at the laundry, but I assumed she was having a tough day. I was keenly aware that my reaction was another testament to my new consciousness that kept me (most of the time) from taking everything personally. I later learned that Emily and Hannah met up to walk the Camino to celebrate their 60th birthdays. There was another twist: They had not seen each other since their high school graduation.

I turned around and spotted Marion in the hall as she passed our room. I was astonished to see that she and Ian were still matching our pace. Gitta's work must have held Marion's blisters in check. Later, the four of us had a tasty Italian meal at the only place in town in a new building. It was more than an hour before we were served, drawing complaints from several patrons in the crowded dining room. Marion described her love of France, where she lived for years. As she talked, I imagined that if she had lived in America as a young woman, she would have looked perfect in a VW bus (with flowers painted on it) driving through Haight Ashbury in San Francisco. I had no doubt it would have been a blast to ride shotgun.

When we returned to our albergue, the common room downstairs had become a campground. Sleeping bags, backpacks, and trekkers blanketed the floor. I asked one young English guy I had talked with on the trail what was going on.

"The place is full, so they let us use the floor since it was so late. It saved us a two-hour walk to the next albergue." I felt fortunate to have a bed, even in a tiny, crowded room.

I slid into my quiet, dimly lit dorm, where the four young people ignored my "*Buenas noches.*" Emily and Hannah were asleep, and it was only 9 p.m.

I kissed Sue good night and crawled into my sleeping bag. Despite aches, I had trekked 70 miles, carrying a backpack, more miles than I had ever walked at once. And the journey was just getting started.

A Santiago

12

Did She Really Say That?

"What was that?" I squinted, still half asleep.

The lights in our dorm had flashed on, and the four young hot shots were out of bed. It was still dark outside. The two men and two women finished getting dressed and rushed to roll up sleeping bags.

"Turn off the f- - -ing light!"

That was Emily, in the bed next to mine.

"Sorry," apologized an offender as she switched off the light and turned on a flashlight.

The four noisily finished packing and dragged their backpacks out the door, which slammed shut behind them.

Emily had another dart in her arsenal. "Good riddance!"

It was 5 a.m., but that was the end of my sleep. I had not heard Sue stir, so, like Emily, she must have gone back to sleep.

I imagined that the four young bunkmates were likely among the trekkers who raced through the Camino. When "racers" passed us on the trail, they were noisy, usually not friendly, and exuded superiority. At bar stops and during meals, some bragged about averaging 25 miles and even more. In his guidebook, John Brierley bemoans those who make the walk a "sporting achievement." He suggests taking six weeks for "a deepening of the experience."

Brierley's guidebook, carried by nearly everyone we saw, divided the Camino into 33 stages. The guidebook was indispensable for us, but I wondered why Brierley didn't divide it into more stages to encourage trekkers to take more time. Sure, the stages were not meant to be followed religiously, but there was subconscious pressure to at least keep up with the book. That led to crowds at most end-of-stage stops. We faced 25 more stages and about 380 miles to Santiago, so we would need to average about 15 miles a day. Add three or four rest days, a couple days in Santiago, a day to get to Madrid and at least a day in Madrid. Our flight from Madrid left in five weeks. That left little wiggle room.

I remembered my vow to take the Camino one day at a time, but I found it impossible to ignore the numbers. We hobbled with painful joints and muscles at the start of each day, but our legs had strengthened, and Sue's wrapping was keeping her feet in check. I was determined not to take a bus to skip a section and felt we would be able to walk farther each day the rest of the way.

The four early birds were likely in Najera, six miles away, when Sue awoke about 7 a.m. By then, I had convinced myself we could make it to Santo Domingo, the end of the upcoming stage, 19 miles away. One long day would make a difference, and we would be in no danger of sharing a room with the "hot shots," who likely would travel well beyond Santo Domingo. I pitched the idea to Sue, who was skeptical. "Let's see how it goes." I should have listened to Gitta's wisdom: "never more than 12 miles a day."

"Good morning, Reg." It was Emily, who stretched her arms and yawned. It already seemed normal to wake up next to a woman I had just met. Not exactly next to, but close.

"Hi, Emily. Did you get back to sleep?" I knew she must have, because her mood had lightened.

"I did, but I hope the four asshats have blisters by now!" Asshats? I had never heard that one. Any pilgrim guilty of disturbing Emily's sleep was in for an earful.

As we ate yogurt and sipped instant coffee in the albergue kitchen, Sue visited with a young Danish woman sitting next to us. She was naturally beautiful without a speck of makeup. "No one should look that good in the morning on the Camino," Sue grumbled later.

Packing renewed energy, we stepped out of the albergue about 8:30 for our seventh day. Snow-capped peaks appeared southwest of us. Except for crossing the N-120, the morning walk through farmland and down into the historic small city of Nájera was relaxing. We drank coffee outside a bar in the usual plastic chairs, which, for the time being, had replaced my leather mission chair at home for welcome rests. Fellow trekkers provided the morning entertainment as they marched by, greeting us with "Hola!" and "Buen Camino!" We saw no familiar faces, but we felt like we knew everyone.

When we rejoined the trail, we climbed briefly to a plain, where we traveled in sunshine until lunchtime. There was no shade in sight, so we settled ourselves on short grass next to a narrow tractor path. A refreshing breeze bent the deep green stalks of grain in alluring, undulating patterns over the slopes as the temperature approached 80. We pulled off our shoes and socks, exposing four feet that celebrated the fresh air. While we ate our crackers, cheese, and apple slices, I scanned the green fields under the deep blue sky.

"It's nice today to not be crisscrossing the highway as much." The trail intersected the N-111 10 times the previous day.

Sue's question came out of nowhere. "Are you ever tempted to put out your thumb on the highway?"

"Not yet, but would I accept a ride if offered? Probably not, but if it gets much warmer, and if the car had AC…"

Sue pointed down the trail. "Uh-oh. Here comes Brenda."

About 100 yards away, an American we had seen several times approached briskly. Brenda was traveling alone and had walked with Sue a couple of times while I ambled ahead, but within their sight.

"What do you mean, 'uh-oh?'"

"After we talked for at least a half hour yesterday, Brenda complained that she had not met any interesting people on the trek that day. She said the sheep made better conversation partners."

"Did she really say that? Are you sure she meant to include you?"

"I think she's shopping for a boyfriend."

As Brenda, from Wisconsin, approached, her long blond hair looked like she had just brushed it. Eye makeup, rarely seen on the Camino, was obviously part of her morning routine.

"You guys chose a great spot for a picnic. Do you want me to take your picture?"

If I had known her better, I might have blurted out my answer with a request.

"Sure, could you get that ram behind me in the photo? He's quite the conversationalist." Sue may not have been fond of Brenda, but she seemed nice enough to me.

Out loud, Sue said, "Yes, thank you."

We chatted with Brenda (she acted interested) while we ate, and I pictured people on the Camino by themselves. Safety was a concern, although most trekkers stayed within shouting (or whistle) distance of others. Boredom was another issue, but Brenda was often walking and talking with others (although they were boring to talk to).

If a solo pilgrim wanted trekking partners, it was easy to find welcoming people. There was plenty of time for solitude, too, no matter how you traveled. Sue and I often had not walked next to each other and trekked long stretches without talking. (I didn't tell Brenda, but I "baaed" at the sheep a few times. Really.) During almost a week, I had rarely been bored. I hadn't once listened to my music playlist. The sounds, sights, and people had been enough. There was ample time to daydream, another journey unto itself. The trek was doing things for me that medication, counseling, and even hypnosis had failed to do. I hoped it would last for the rest of the way (or even my life).

After lunch, we shared our large chocolate bar with Brenda. "Chocolate is one of the best parts of the Camino," I said as I chewed. She looked at me like I was nuts before she hurried back to the trail. I put on my still-sweaty socks (the same ones I wore the day before) and wedged my feet into my shoes, which I kept as far away from my nose as I could.

An hour later, it was in the low 80s and still no shade in sight as we approached the uphill trail to Cirueña, which perched at about

2,400 feet. A helmeted bicyclist pulled up, dismounted, and introduced himself.

For a moment, I wondered if I had a sign on my back: "Please stop and talk to us!" But the bicyclist's action was anything but unusual for this pilgrimage. He sounded American and wore a tattered, sweat-soaked t-shirt and shorts. The old hybrid looked big for him.

"Where are you from, Paul?"

"Michigan. I'm doing a study abroad in Grenada, and it's spring break."

"It must be tough to carry a backpack while you are riding. What brought you so far north?"

"A Spanish friend at school told me about the Camino. I bought this bike in Pamplona and fixed it up." The bike looked like it had been pulled off a junk pile, except for the newish tires.

After climbing about a third of the way up the hill, we paused for a drink of water. Paul bent his head back and splashed water on his face.

"How far are you going?" I asked.

"Santiago, I hope. I have eight days to get there."

"How do you get past the rocky parts?" Sue asked.

"Oh, I just carry my bike. There are some other paths for bikes too."

Paul's easy conversation distracted us from the challenging climb on the scorching-hot cinder path. As he jumped back on his bike and accelerated away, Sue looked at me and expressed my thoughts: "He must be stronger than he looks."

Paul seemed self-assured. When I was in college, I was nowhere near as confident. I was the first on either side of my family to attend college, and it showed. Two part-time jobs gave me an excuse to avoid my awkwardness around other college students, except for a small group of friends that dwindled after my first year.

I had considered skipping college and accepting an offer to continue the newspaper sports-writing job I held during my senior year of high school. Thankfully, reason won. College would cost me nothing, since financial need and grades brought a full ride. Mostly, I knew Mom would be crushed if I didn't go to college.

I watched Paul pedal into the distance and remembered my first trip to UCSB with a high school friend. I wanted to see the place where I would spend the next four years. I had applied to only UCSB because it was close to my hometown. Few people would believe that I could have been so clueless about college.

As we drove through the campus, I noticed there were enough buildings—including some eight stories tall—to make a small city.

"Which part is UCSB?" I asked.

My friend laughed like I was joking around. He looked at me for a smile and realized my question was serious.

"Reg, really?"

Reality still eluded me.

"I feel weird saying this, Reg, but all of this is UCSB."

We were both bewildered. I tried to act cool, like I knew it all along, but he wasn't fooled.

A few years later, my high school friend told me what he remembered about my naiveté.

"I didn't know whether to laugh it off or cry, Reg."

I had befriended more people during my short time on the Camino than during my college career. After a moderately social second half of my freshman year, I immersed myself in my part-time jobs and spent little of my limited spare time socializing with fellow students. I made good friends through my jobs, but some probably wondered why I wasn't with my peers more often. I was seldom comfortable at UCSB. I worried that I would appear outclassed by more worldly classmates if I allowed my real self to show.

As a father, I hoped that sons Brad, Chris, and Andrew would be better adjusted than I had been, admittedly not a high bar. Sue and I provided them with stable lives and diverse experiences. They lived in a neighborhood with about 20 other kids for nearly their entire childhoods. They played t-ball, soccer, and basketball. We installed a basketball court and swimming pool, and our house became a neighborhood magnet. Family dinners were a religion, as was family travel, including a year living in Scotland when I was selected for a teaching exchange.

A few minutes after Paul sped away, I wanted to yell, "Hey, Paul, I know three young men who can do anything you can do."

Hot and sweaty, we finally reached the tiny hilltop village of Cirueña, where we stopped for a break in the small plaza. There was Marion, sitting in the shade of a bar umbrella.

"Hi, Marion. Where's Ian?" I said.

"He's walking. My feet flared up, so I took a bus."

"I'm sorry to hear that. Are you staying here?"

"Yes, in a small Catholic albergue. It's a bit strange, but it's probably all right. Are you going to stay here?"

I looked at Sue. We had come more than 14 miles, and there were between four and five more to Santo Domingo, a city with several accommodations.

I scanned the lonely outpost. "We were thinking of going to Santo Domingo." Cirueña felt uncomfortable, and Marion had not made the albergue sound very good. I imagined Catholic nuns requiring prayer and evening hymn sing-alongs.

Marion scrunched up her brow and shook her head. "That's a long way, and it's hot."

Either the heat affected our judgment or we were swayed by the probability of staying in a nicer place, but we decided to push on. It would not take long for us to regret it.

We gulped cold lemonade with Marion before heading downhill toward Santo Domingo. Within a half hour Sue's toes were overheating on the trail. We stopped, and she let her feet get some air, then she rewrapped. Sue was struggling, and as I watched her pain and frustration grow, it became clear we should have stopped in Cirueña. I applied an adhesive patch to the ball of my right foot to prevent a hot spot from becoming a blister, aware that I had it easy compared to Sue. Our competitive nature had led us astray on our seventh day, and it would not be the last time.

When we finally dragged into Santo Domingo de la Calzada (89 miles in seven days), we stopped at the first albergue, the four-story, 162-bed Casa del Santo operated by the Spanish Confraternity, a Christian volunteer organization. We received a warm welcome at the office downstairs. I was hoping for the peace of a private room, but the women at the front desk said the albergue didn't have any.

"We have some dorm beds left."

That was not going to cut it for me. I turned away from the women and faced Sue.

"Let's try somewhere else."

"I'm not going anywhere," Sue snapped. "My feet are killing me. What happened to gratitude?"

Our hosts squirmed and sent us to the fourth floor, where the small dorm held several bunks. They may have taken pity on us after a long, hot day. Or, they wanted us as far away as possible. The charge was a donation of the customer's choice. We had heard religious hostels operated that way. Some said they were "free." Others would say, "Be generous."

As I rested on my lower bunk, I reflected on how I had acted in front of the women at the front desk. It was a big place, and they were working hard. It was a clean, nice facility run mostly by volunteers. But I had let my exhaustion overrule common sense. We waited for others to take the empty beds in our room, but no one came, so it turned out to be a big private room after all.

A note on the bulletin board at the albergue offered a free service: foot first aid. Sue found a young man (who she referred to as the handsome young Spaniard) waiting downstairs. He worked on an oozing blister on her left pinkie toe, and she said she felt much better. We hoped it would last. He lent some foot care advice, and she insisted he accept a cash donation. Afterward, he grabbed his helmet and roared off on his motorcycle, his long dark hair dangling out of his helmet in the wind. To complete the bad-boy picture, he wore tight, faded blue jeans. Sue may have imagined herself riding on the back of his motorcycle (all the way to Santiago!). I didn't feel jealous, but I did wish I looked that good in tight jeans. I wondered (very briefly) if I should grow my hair long.

Santo Domingo, a city of 5,600, was dedicated to the memory of Dominic de la Calzada, whose efforts nearly a thousand years ago brought a hospital, bridge, paths, church and hotels for pilgrims. The hospital was converted to a modern, luxury Parador Hotel. Santo

Domingo offered several restaurants and bars in an inviting downtown plaza, where we found ourselves after a slow walk from the albergue. I stepped inside a bar, and as I ordered drinks, I greeted a man in his 60s who sat next to the door. A Belgian, he was walking his second solo Camino in two years.

"Why are you doing it again?"

"I needed it." He pointed at his head. "It brings me peace and makes me fit."

After just a week, I could understand. As tough as the seventh day had been, I felt comfort in the rhythm and simplicity of life on the trail.

Sue and I settled into a table outside the bar, soothed by the cooler early evening air. In 10 days, Santo Domingo would host its annual two-week fiesta, and I imagined how the beautiful medieval architecture and narrow streets would bring authenticity to the party. I thought how the city would make the perfect setting for a movie about pilgrims 500 years (or more) ago.

"How do your feet feel?" I wondered.

"Much better, and the foot therapist was good for my eyes too. Today was a tough day."

"Paul, the bicyclist, is a brave kid. I was floored that a guy so young took the time to stop and walk with us. Maybe because we are American."

"Aren't you paying attention, honey? Can't you feel the bonds we all share? Almost everyone is struggling in some way, but we keep going. Paul was drawn to us because he wanted to share his Camino with us. And he knew we would want to hear his story. His age and being American don't matter."

A familiar voice rang out from my right.

"Sue. Reg!"

It was Gert, the German we met over dinner at the village below the castle on our third day. We had talked to him over the past several days while we passed each other. He packed a sturdy frame, graying hair, and a deeply tanned face. I felt like I was seeing an old friend for the first time in a long while.

"How are you, Gert?"

He looked relieved and sighed as he sat at our table. He was one of many men who grew beards on the trek. I was among the few who shaved every day.

"I am okay, but my feet, they hurt."

Gert had been doctoring blisters for the past two days. He took off his glasses and wiped them on the sleeve of his shirt.

"I will be all right. I need to go now and find a bed. I see you soon!"

He disappeared around the corner with a slight limp.

I thought back to what Sue had said about Paul. She was right. The Camino wasn't about getting to Santiago. It wasn't about the miles we traveled. The journey was about people and the adventures we shared. It was about testing our limits, separately and together.

Sue put it another way. "This is a fellowship."

13

It Hurt Like Crazy

It was the dawn of our second week on the Camino de Santiago, and as Sue slept in the bunk above, I contemplated what brought me here. When we watched Martin Sheen's movie eight months before, I had dismissed the idea of walking the Camino: "We can't do that!"

Sue's response, "But what if we can?" had new meaning after my first week in Spain.

I had arrived in Pamplona with a catalog of fears. As I lay on my bunk bed at the four-story Christian hostel, I wondered what my friend Ron would have said about my Camino anxieties. I have heard his voice many times since his death.

"I guarantee you, Reg, after a couple of days, those worries will be history. Listen to Sue. I've always known she was the brains in your family."

Ron would have been correct on both counts. I never sensed that he stewed over much, except occasionally his job. But he cared about his family and friends, so I expect he would have said more.

"Reg, let me tell ya. Why are you even thinking about things you can't control? Focus on your adventure with your wife. Now, let's have another beer, my friend."

I vowed to often travel my brain's path to his words of wisdom. It was a bit early for a beer, though, so I hoped Ron wouldn't mind waiting until happy hour.

In *The Way*, Sheen's character (Tom) walks with three trekkers in their thirties and forties who are quick to share their reasons for hiking the Camino. Joost, who is Dutch, wants to lose weight to make his wife happier. Sarah, from Canada, vows to quit smoking at the end of the trail. Jack, an Irishman, fights writer's block as he tries to finish a book about the Camino. Tom, a widower, copes with the grief of losing his only child. By the end of the movie, they transcend their problems to grow in ways they had not foreseen. Jack says, "No one walks the Camino by accident."

When people reach the front of the compostela line at the Camino office in Santiago, a clerk asks them why they walked. Those who say it was at least partly for religious or spiritual reasons earn the regular certificate in Latin. Trekkers who say, "To find a girlfriend," or "Hey, it's a cheap way to travel" receive a different certificate, written in Spanish. Whether or not they are legitimate pilgrims is a common subject of debate.

I wondered about my answer. When I began my journey, my goal was to conquer my fears and walk all the way to Santiago. I would have been issued a compostela in Spanish.

"If I am fortunate enough to make it to Santiago, what will I say?" I imagined as Sue stirred in the bunk above. I wasn't sure yet exactly how I would answer. But a week into the pilgrimage, I knew my compostela would be written in Latin.

Our 14 miles to Belorado would be shorter, less picturesque and cooler than the previous day. As dark clouds hovered, I zipped up my rain jacket and draped the rain fly over my pack. We would hug the busy N-120 most of the day. Just out of the day's starting gate, we turned a corner and looming above us was a large sign beckoning trekkers to call and reserve a room at the Pensión Toni in Belorado.

So far, we had taken our chances and found beds in albergues at the end of each day. I had overheard several pilgrims say that making reservations was against the spirit of the Camino. Purists always stayed in albergue dorms. I respected that attitude, but I was not that strong. I resisted admitting I might have been sympathetic to another view: It is my Camino.

I looked up at the advertisement and pictured the luxury of private lodging. "Should I call and see if they have a room?"

I expected Sue to suggest that we hold off, but she surprised me. "Sure, if you are ready with Spanish in case they don't speak English."

My Spanish was good enough, and the friendly proprietor promised "*con el baño*" (with a bathroom). Although beds had been plentiful so far, it was a relief to know we would walk into Belorado with a room secured.

Three climbs took us to about 2,600 feet. As on many sections, there were several albergues in villages every two or three miles for those who wanted to avoid crowds by finding between-stage accommodations. In a few days, we would cross into the meseta, known for being bleak, without shade, and blistering hot in summer.

Belorado, a town of 2,100, was built around a plaza with a rustic church tower and castle ruins on a hill above. The cool, damp weather was probably responsible for the deserted streets as we arrived. We had reached triple figures: 103 miles in eight days, 350 to go. Our pensión room was grandmotherly in decor, but comfortable, and the manager offered to do our laundry, albeit for the pricey €12. We were in no mood to wash, rinse and hang, so we handed over a bagful. The anticipated smell of machine-washed clothes was too tempting.

A welcome e-mail got our attention. It was Ian and Marion; they were in a hotel in Belorado. We joined them for cocktails next to the roaring stone fireplace and enjoyed the rustic charm of their hotel.

"How are your feet, Marion?" I had to ask.

"They still hurt."

I wondered what it would take for them to quit and return to England. Ian was a fast walker and experienced adventure traveler, but I could imagine him pushing himself too hard. I saw several strong trekkers who were forced to return home. Marion had compromised by taking the bus, but I did not sense defeat, at least not yet. She wasn't thrilled about waiting around at the next village until Ian arrived. The trek had not gone how they hoped, and I sensed their frustration. They so badly wanted to get to Santiago, but they also didn't want to miss the social and even, perhaps, the spiritual experiences.

The four of us enjoyed an Italian dinner at a deserted restaurant. In fact, the entire town was dead, which was unusual for an end-of-stage village. When we returned to our room, our laundry was neatly stacked on the bed. Sue picked up a shirt and smelled the freshness.

"Can you believe this service?" As she separated my clothes into another stack, she found her underwear.

"What happened? These used to be pink, white, and blue."

Not any more; Sue would wear gray panties the rest of the way. From experience, I knew what had happened. I rolled my eyes, expecting Sue to protest further, but she took it in stride. Not long after we were married, I once mixed our darks and whites, as I had done to my clothes for years of bachelorhood. My punishment was a lifetime ban from doing laundry (one that I have never protested); this guy got €12.

In the morning, I looked out the window, hoping the cold, wet weather of the previous day had passed. No such luck. In fact, if the guy on the street below was any indication, it was even colder. He wore thick gloves, a heavy raincoat, and his breath was visible as he held his crossed arms against his chest. My legs protested as I strode across our room. On day nine, trekking sounded terrible. It would not be the last time.

Sue was taping her toes.

"How do they feel?"

"They hurt, especially between my two little toes."

I pitched the idea of a rest day.

"But what are we going to do here all day? Sit in our room? It is too cold and wet to be tourists. We might as well walk." I was hoping she would say that.

It was near freezing with light rain when our shoes hit the pavement. We wore several layers, including raincoats over down jackets, but the damp cold chilled to the bone. Gloves and wide-brimmed waterproof hats were saviors.

Seven miles later we arrived at a crowded bar at Villafranca Montes de Oca and quickly decided we would splurge and eat lunch indoors. A mix of locals and pilgrims filled the bar, and we waved to Americans Emily and Hannah, who were huddled in serious conversation over the guidebook.

Spanish bars were beacons of comfort. When we didn't get breakfast at our lodging, they were our go-to stop for coffee, juice and either thick toast or a slice of *tortilla de patatas*, if it was offered. We had gotten spoiled by a second coffee mid-morning and even an afternoon bar coffee after our picnic lunches. Happy hour followed showers and we depended on bars for dinner when albergues did not offer meals.

The Villafranca bar was warm, with an unusually big deli section. I spied large slabs of jamón hanging behind the counter, so I ordered some, thinly sliced, with cheese, on a small baguette. Tasty, but I needed two glasses of water to wash down the crusty bread. I watched a truck pull up near the front door. The heavyset, bearded driver swung open the door, greeted the bar keeper, who slid an espresso shot across the bar. The driver drank it like a shot of tequila, left a coin, and was back in his truck in about a minute. Spanish bars offered something for everyone.

As we finished lunch, Sue summed up our situation. "So, it's eight miles to San Juan de Ortega. We could stay at an albergue here."

"But the albergues won't open for several hours. What are we going to do all afternoon? I wish there was somewhere else to stay between here and San Juan."

"So, here we are again. Do we sit inside for hours, or just walk?"

Sue's feet needed a rest day, but we wanted to save it for an interesting place. We decided to tackle the eight miles to San Juan and knew there would be no bars on the way. The guidebook showed three climbs for a total of 1,500 feet to an elevation of 3,500. The light rain was intermittent. The Arctic-like chill was gone, but it was still only in the mid-forties.

The path out of the village stretched straight as an arrow, steeply uphill, over rocky terrain to a gravel road through dense oak and pine forest. A roller coaster of hills stretched as far as I could see. We saw only two other trekkers the entire afternoon. The hours felt like days until, aching to the bone, we finally limped into San Juan de Ortega in late afternoon. The village of 30 people offered a hostel that we had read was cold and drafty. There was a church and a bar. And what was that?

Sue was hopeful. "A pensión?"

We entered the modern building through a glass-paneled door, revealing a large room with tables and a kitchen. Opposite was a hallway with a series of doors.

I was confident. "This has to be a pensión."

We waited a few minutes for a sign of life. Sue suggested we inquire at the bar across the road.

Minutes later I held a key to an en suite room. We were elated and thankful that we could afford the upgrade from the albergue. When we opened the door to the warm room, Sue fell backwards onto the comfy queen-sized bed, closed her eyes, and exhaled relief.

"That was hell!"

When she removed her socks and toe wrappings, we were dispirited by what we saw. Her small toes as well as the sides of her heels and balls of her feet looked like they were covered with blood-red bubble wrap. I could hardly stand to look. Sue was running out of gauze and tape, and we would not find a pharmacy in the tiny village, but she managed to bandage the worst areas. For the second straight day, reason had lost to our competitive nature, and I feared the consequences.

Fortunately, drinks and dinner beckoned in the bar a few steps away, across the deserted road. Next to a crackling fireplace, we found Huan and Linda, the Canadians from the underpass party who sat with Gert. We would not have felt more welcome if we had entered our own living room.

Sue and I ordered glasses of Tempranillo.

Gert was becoming a regular on our Camino. "Sue, your feet. They feel better than mine?" His English was good, but he sometimes skipped words.

"Well, Gert, we could take off our shoes to compare, but I would rather just drink."

Time to change the subject.

"Reg, I have a surprise for you."

"What is it, Linda?"

"It is outside the bar, across the street. Look for a door with a window."

Huan laughed as I left the bar.

Linda had piqued my curiosity. Across the courtyard, I found a tiny room with a window in the door. I peered inside.

"What? Oooh, that looks comfy," I surmised when I saw the coin-operated massage chair. I tugged on the handle and the door opened. I fished in my pocket and found 50 cents. Before I inserted the coins, my eyes scanned the room for a camera, and I wondered if it was a set up. The coins clinked in, I put my arms and legs in four padded sleeves, and waited. The sleeves inflated, the chair vibrated. I closed my eyes, put my head back, and loved every second. It was the perfect cure for my angry muscles. "Thank you, Linda!" I wanted to yell. I immediately reached in my pocket and found another 50 cents, my last coins.

My unselfish side interrupted before I could drop the coins into the machine. "Don't you dare, Reg. Sue would love this."

I returned to the bar, where Huan and Linda laughed when they saw me. I broke into a broad smile. I told Sue and Gert about the chair, and Sue looked at me suspiciously. But she took the 50 cents anyway and hobbled out of the bar to the magic chair. Gert played it safe and stayed with his beer. Traveling by himself, I had watched him blend in with various groups of pilgrims of many ages. I had listened to him speak Spanish as well as German and English. Everyone liked Gert, who made friends in a quiet, welcoming manner.

The toasty fire roared in the fireplace.

Huan was curious. "We didn't see you in the albergue."

I tried not to sound smug. "We lucked out across the road."

"You're lucky. The albergue is even worse than the guidebook says. Cold showers. No heat. But we have beds."

Gert didn't have much good to say either. "The mattress is on the floor. It is freezing. Maybe I will sleep here in the bar."

We were thinking about what to order for dinner when Sue returned.

"Wasn't it great?" I asked.

I saw right away that Sue didn't agree. "What do you mean? The sleeves squeezed my legs so tightly that I thought my toes were going to explode. It hurt like crazy; I couldn't pull my legs out or stop the machine! It just kept squeezing and squeezing."

I was glad Gert, Huan, and Linda were at the table to diffuse Sue's frustration, and we ended up laughing so hard that we shed tears, releasing the tension of the day. But beneath the laughter, I felt bad that my idea to make Sue feel better had backfired.

After a satisfying dinner of salad and hearty soup, Huan and Linda were off to the pilgrim mass in the chapel. Gert remained in the bar, next to the fireplace, when we bid him good night.

We returned to our warm room with little suspicion about what the next day held.

FARMACIA

14

Should We Call an Ambulance?

Sue and I slid into the back of the grungy, unmarked taxi, desperate to get to Burgos. Our driver hopped in, nearly dropping the cigarette that dangled from his mouth. His seat slammed into my knees.

"*A donde*?" (Where to?), he asked as if he was yelling to a drunk he had just picked up. I wondered why he had not closed the trunk, which held everything we owned.

Suddenly, out of nowhere, a sedan screeched to a halt in front of us, its flashing blue lights forcing me to squint. Sky-blue doors sprung open, revealing a pair of uniformed police officers who wore faces that made it clear they concluded they had arrived at a crime scene.

Our driver leaped out, tossed his cigarette aside and faced the officer who towered over him. He shouted at the dark uniform in Spanish.

Sue and I exchanged shocked looks as my car door flew open, and the second officer waved for us to get out. Faster than we could ask "*Que pasa*?" (What's happening?), the officer who had opened my door yanked our red backpacks from the trunk and tossed them to the ground.

We stood in shock, wondering what was next.

As his partner argued with the driver, the shorter officer eyed us with his hands on his hips.

"*Estás bien*?" (Are you okay?)

Once the officer's words sunk in, my relief was mixed with confusion.

Before I could answer the officer, Alex, who had served us dinner the night before, emerged from the nearby bar and approached the police. He and the shorter officer exchanged a few sentences in Spanish before Alex stood before Sue and me.

"You are lucky," he said.

"What do you mean?" I asked.

"The police saved you from a long, expensive ride. The driver is unlicensed and cheats customers, especially foreigners."

I told Alex about Sue's foot and the maintenance worker who called the "taxi" for us. He shook his head, closed his eyes and squeezed his lower jaw with his left hand.

"I am sorry this has happened. I will call a real taxi for you right now."

A half hour earlier, in our pensión room, four words from Sue got my attention.

"Honey, look at this."

My heart fell when I saw her left foot. The front third was bright red and blisters had left her toes fleshy and bloody.

"I think it's infected."

"We need to get you to a doctor right away."

"Burgos is not far, and there has to be a hospital there."

"Should we call an ambulance?"

"I think a taxi would be all right."

"But I'm not sure how to call a taxi in Spanish."

After a few moments of near-panic, I had an idea.

"I'll try to find someone who can call one for us. Be right back."

I hurried across the road to the albergue, found a short, plump maintenance worker and told him, *"Mi esposa esta enferma y tiene que ir al medica."* (My wife is sick and has to go to the doctor.) That is what I wanted to say in Spanish, at least. I made enough sense that he got the idea and pulled out his cell phone to call for a taxi.

The real taxi, equipped with a meter and company signs, arrived before I could grasp the morning. The fake taxi incident had awakened the sleepy village with a flurry of screeching tires, flashing lights, slamming car doors, and yelling. The officers continued to talk to the "fake" driver across the courtyard. I wondered how long it would take to get to a hospital. I hoped the driver was dependable, and that Sue could see a doctor without the endless waits we had faced in California emergency rooms. The taxi driver lifted our backpacks into the trunk and pointed for us to get into the back seat. I hoped we would remember the Spanish we had rehearsed.

"Where do you need to go?" Marco asked. That settled the language challenge.

"The hospital," Sue directed.

It was mid-morning on a cool Saturday as we drove the 15 miles into Burgos, a beautiful city of 170,000 on the Arlanzon River.

Marco, the driver, told us the Hospital Universitario had a strong reputation. While he drove, he tried to teach Sue how to say, "I have a blister on my little toe." (*Tengo una ampolla en mi pequeño dedo del pie.*) Each time she repeated it, he said, "No, no," followed by a chuckle. Sue's efforts sounded like a different language than Marco was speaking. His patient, light-hearted approach distracted us and calmed our nerves.

As Marco steered the taxi into the Hospital Universitario emergency room entrance, my gut told me I could trust our young driver. He was not confident about Sue's Spanish, though, so he walked with us to the ER counter, where a woman in a white uniform greeted us in Spanish. Marco explained the situation as Sue and I listened gratefully. He turned to us, bid us "Buen Camino" and drove off before I could say more than "Muchas gracias!" I wished I could have had the chance for a proper display of appreciation. Sue would have hugged him. An alert uniformed security guard locked our backpacks in a storage room as we sat in the deserted waiting area.

Minutes later, we were in an examining room with a doctor who was pleasant but spoke little English. The large room was filled with gleaming hardware, and the doctor was old enough to have had a couple decades of medical experience. He held Sue's foot in his hands, shook his head, and said, "*Infección! Si, es calor.*" (Infection. It is hot.) He used Google translate through a computer monitor next to the patient bed to tell us about the treatment (dressing and antibiotics). He patiently answered our questions through Google, cleaned Sue's blisters, and dressed her foot.

Then he pointed to the monitor, which showed an unexpected translation: "Two days' rest and you may go back to the Camino." I had assumed our walk was over.

As I processed my relief, I flipped to 2011, the last time Sue and I had watched a doctor's computer monitor together. Ultimately, that monitor's picture had a lot to do with our coming to Spain. A neurosurgeon in Fresno had summoned us to see the results of an MRI of Sue's neck. Sue was hoping, finally, for a diagnosis, but she was hardly prepared for what she was about to hear.

"See that?"

We watched as his finger pointed to a white image about the size of a little finger.

"There is a tumor inside your spinal cord that has been causing your numbness. I cannot believe you are still walking."

I felt chills as the doctor explained the surgery.

"I will need to remove a bone in your neck to get into your spinal column. It is very difficult surgery, but must be done soon. Any nerve damage caused by the tumor could be irreversible."

He sounded like an auto mechanic explaining how to repair a car's broken valves.

"If things go well, you will walk out of the hospital. If not, you could be a quadriplegic, or even die."

His tone was still mechanical, but his words were not.

I gripped Sue's hand.

"But if we do nothing, the tumor will kill you."

Sue knew something had been wrong for months, and finally, after several misdiagnoses, she had an answer. But the news was devastating and during the two weeks before the surgery, we lived on a bed of nails.

Surgery day was the longest day of my life. Our oldest son Andrew and his wife Leah had flown from their home in Portland, Oregon. Their presence comforted both of us beyond measure. Son Brad was in France on a study abroad term, and Chris was visiting friends in Nicaragua. I knew the hours would pass slowly for them as well while they awaited word about their mother.

In the prep room, a surgical nurse explained to Sue and me that Sue would be strapped face down to a special gurney that would hold her still. The nurse said she would monitor Sue's sensory responses and immediately alert the surgeon if she detected a problem that would indicate the scalpel had touched a danger area.

In the waiting room, a message board on the wall showed surgeries in progress. For Sue, it read "In surgery" for the three longest hours I had ever lived. I sat. I paced. I was crazy with worry that the surgeon's knife had been off by a fraction of an inch.

About noon, I checked the message board.

"In recovery."

I tried to imagine what that would mean. Would she walk out of the hospital? Two hours later, no word from the surgeon. The tension was more than I could bear. I found refuge pacing for at least another hour in a deserted hallway, where I eventually sat on the floor, back against the wall, knees holding up my arms, in which I buried my face.

How would I react if Sue was paralyzed for life? How would Sue handle it? How could I go on without her if she didn't survive? How would I tell my sons?

"Mr. Spittle?"

I raised my face from my arms when I recognized the surgeon's voice. I stood and looked into his eyes, seeking a sign. His face was serious, no hint of a smile.

"We got the tumor out safely, and it was benign. There was no further damage during the surgery. Your wife should be fine."

When I found Andrew and Leah in the waiting room, we shared relief and hugs. I quickly contacted Brad and Chris with the news. More calls brought comfort to other family members and friends.

Sue's narrow escape was a major factor leading to our early retirement the following year. We vowed to live full lives, especially when it came to travel.

Slightly more than a year after the tumor was removed, Sue had brought us to Spain, where her strength and determination would allow us to continue our journey after another difficult test. She would need to monitor her foot carefully, and the Burgos doctor directed her to have it checked at a clinic in a few days.

Back at the ER front desk, the woman who had registered Sue less than an hour before offered to call a taxi. While we waited for our ride, the security guard brought our backpacks and wished us "Buen Camino." Many thoughtful Spaniards had entered our lives during the morning: the police officers, the bartender at the albergue, Marco the taxi driver, the woman at the ER desk, the hospital security guard, and, of course, the doctor. They were superheroes to me. Sue had been calm and brave while I had tested my cardiovascular and nervous systems.

The taxi (I had checked when it arrived that it had a meter and official signage.) took us to the Acuarela Hostal, a hotel that Marco had recommended. We spotted a pharmacy's bright green sign nearby and collected Sue's prescription before we checked into the hotel. Sue wore her Teva sandals and was able to walk short distances slowly. At the pharmacy counter, the cashier took Sue's prescription, opened a drawer, and gave Sue the antibiotics in exchange for €10. We were in the store just a couple of minutes.

The Acuarela Hostal was like modern, boutique hotels in California. An elevator took us to our small room on the third floor. It was our only elevator in Spain, and it came when Sue needed it most. We rinsed out clothes, hung them around the room, and Sue settled into an afternoon of reading and resting. My relief still felt raw as I considered the traumatic morning.

In Spain, Sue didn't need to spend all day in an emergency room to get good care. Marco the taxi driver, and others eclipsed the call of duty and made sure she got what she needed.

"The Camino will provide." I had heard it many times. It was not the last time we would benefit from its promise.

15

Sorry, Charlie

Sue propped her head against a pillow on the double bed. Sunlight flooded our Burgos hotel room through the large window. House Hunters buyers would have called the bathroom up to date, even luxurious. We paid €60 per night, the most expensive lodging on our Camino, but it included breakfast in the glass-roofed atrium.

It was early afternoon as we settled into our room.

"I think my heartbeat is normal for the first time in hours. How is your foot?"

"Better, but I am wiped out. Maybe the antibiotics will help me sleep."

"Do you need anything? I'm going to look for snacks and dinner possibilities."

"That sounds good."

It was ten minutes to downtown Burgos, filled with bars, restaurants, and shops in the three- and four-story buildings that dominated. Families walked the streets; children held parents' and grandparents' hands. Teen-agers paraded in groups, cradled their cell phones, and laughed, just being kids. A typical Saturday afternoon, I presumed. I wished several groups of backpack-toting trekkers "Buen Camino." My sandals and socks were giveaways that I was a fellow pilgrim. A deli offered bread and cheese for a snack, plus bottled soda, a treat. I ventured another couple of blocks into the central city before tracking back to our hotel carrying our late lunch.

Sue was still asleep as I sat in a desk chair next to the bed, eating fresh bread and tasty, soft Burgos cheese, a local specialty made with sheep's milk. As I replayed the morning's crazy events, I knew we had been lucky. Sue was going to be all right. One day we would laugh about the illegal taxi. My belief in the Camino was stronger than ever. It was not a religious journey for me, but my heart was filled with a new sensation. Was it spiritual? Was it faith?

It wouldn't be the Camino without more unexpected events, one coming just minutes after Sue awoke.

"Honey, look at this!"

Sue stared at her iPad screen, not her foot, thankfully. She had awakened, eaten bread and cheese, and logged onto Wi-Fi to check e-mail. I looked over her shoulder.

"Reg and Sue. Where are you? We just checked into an albergue in Burgos."

It was Ian and Marion, who, thankfully, would not leave us alone.

We reunited with the Oxford, England duo in a noisy bar across the expansive plaza from the Burgos cathedral. We sipped gin and tonics (Lemonade for Sue) at a cramped table next to large windows with views of the 13th century Gothic cathedral, whose spires climbed from two huge towers. It was early Saturday evening, still hours from dinner for most Spaniards, and Ian had the first question.

"Now, Reg and Sue, what mischief have you two been up to?"

I glanced at Sue, who gazed at her left foot. I took a deep breath and shook my head.

"Where do you want me to start? Illegal taxi, the police, or the hospital?"

Ian laughed, thinking I had to be joking. Marion had worry written all over her face.

We were on our second drinks by the time we got caught up. Ian and Marion shared concern for Sue's foot, but Ian helped us find reasons to laugh about the day's shenanigans.

"You Americans, always making trouble."

"That's why you can't resist following us, Ian. We give you boring Brits something to talk about."

Later, the Englishman introduced me to the world of tapas at a nearby restaurant while Marion and Sue regrettably ate the salty fish from the menu. Ian and I crowded next to the tall counter where trays of tapas awaited our choices. I could barely hear his descriptions over other patrons' laughter and shouted drink orders, but we returned to our table with plates full of tasty bites. My favorite was the *gambas al ajillo*, Spanish garlic shrimp. After dinner, we parted with hugs and vowed to see each other along the trail. Sadly, we would not see Ian and Marion on the Camino again as they leaped ahead during our second rest day. It would not be long before we read Ian's parting e-mail. They had cut their trek short due to injury and had gone home to Oxford. We weren't sure if it was Marion's feet or if Ian got hurt. We were saddened, and I knew they were devastated. Another sobering reminder that, like life, one's Camino can change in an instant.

The next morning, I enjoyed a Sunday stroll around Burgos and returned to our hotel with another shocker in the form of a couple from Denmark.

Gitta was looking at Sue's left foot. "Sue, the doctor did a good job dressing your foot."

"It already feels better than it did yesterday," Sue said.

"I am glad you are staying here at the hotel today. James and I are so sorry about the taxi scam and your infection."

They sat in our hotel lobby with Sue and me on a warm, clear Sunday morning. Minutes earlier I had finished a tour of the Burgos cathedral when I spotted the Danish couple walking hand in hand in the plaza. I shouted "Gitta, James!" After hearing about Sue's foot infection, Gitta insisted that I take them to her right away.

Sue didn't think she would see them again. "I expected you would be back in Copenhagen by now."

"We leave in the morning," James said.

After dinner together in downtown Burgos, James had a parting message. "The Camino will take care of you, but stay away from unmarked taxis."

Ian, Marion, James and Gitta. We had shared just 10 days with them, but our bonding had happened quickly, and it felt like it would last a lifetime, even though we did not share nationalities. The corridor of life that traveled across Spain led to more than I had expected. I would miss our Danish and English friends, but the Camino stretched 300 miles into the unknown with plenty of discoveries ahead.

Sue's foot was much improved after the two-day rest, but we were determined to limit our mileage for a couple of days as we resumed our trek. Seven miles after leaving Burgos on a thinly overcast, but warm day, I sat on a bench with my shoes off in the small village of Rabé de las Calzadas. Sue photographed bright red and yellow tulips covering a circular garden when we noticed a two-story albergue in the plaza. The guidebook said there were 24 beds; dinner and breakfast were offered. Bricks framed the windows, and benches lined the rock wall surrounding the front door, which stood alongside the Camino. A soda machine advertising Coca-Cola stood under a huge yellow arrow. Our next chance for beds was five miles farther.

Sue knew what we should do. "Let's take a chance." It was about 1 p.m., and the albergue would not open for at least two hours, so we parked our packs next to the front door and waited. Our choice would be rewarded with the memory of two words that would mark the day forever.

We had been waiting about 15 minutes when a trekker with a tall backpack rounded the corner on the other side of the plaza.

Sue recognized him immediately. "I think that's Gert!"

We persuaded Gert to stay in the albergue with us. He stacked his backpack behind ours, and the three of us were soon sharing a bottle of red wine outside the bar at the village entrance. After hearing Sue's foot, taxi, and hospital story, Gert had a cure. "More *vino tinto*! (red wine) Sue, I get you drunk; the foot will hurt no more!" He raised his glass and laughed with us. The mild-mannered German had a wilder side, and it was not the last time we would see it.

The afternoon passed quickly and so did another bottle, shared by a second German trekker who happened by. Henrik was about my age and proud of his accomplishments. Twenty miles in six hours, carrying his heavy pack, was one highlight. He waved his arms to animate his stories. I could see that Gert's patience with Henrik's boasting was running out, so we meandered back to the albergue just in time to check in.

The albergue, Libéranos Dómine, filled up quickly, and Sue, Henrik and I found ourselves roommates in a small, three-bunk dorm room upstairs. Gert was assigned a bed in the larger dorm. Henrik stripped to his tight briefs without a stitch of modesty and headed for the shower. I was still getting used to trekkers, usually men, undressing in rooms and parading around the halls in their undies. I had become bolder than I was the first night, even changing from trousers to shorts in the room. That was a big step, but I still didn't walk to the bathroom in my boxer briefs. Even by Americans' prudish standards, I knew I was unusually discrete.

Vicky, a Texan, and her teen-aged brother Tom took the bunk beds across from us. Tom complained about painful blisters, and Vicky was lovingly patient with her brother, who seemed to require extra attention. I sat on my bed across from their bunk as she cleaned his feet, applied ointment and bandages. For a moment, I saw the doctor laboring over Sue's left foot in the hospital.

Vicky wrapped her arm around Tom's shoulders. "I was planning to come to Spain by myself, but I reconsidered when I realized it would be good for him to come along." He basked in his sister's mothering.

Room, dinner, and breakfast at Libéranos Dómine was €20 each, a steal even by Camino standards. The efficient, apron-clad woman running the hostel had checked us in before hurrying back to her kitchen. Later, she impressed us with a delicious, satisfying three-course vegetarian dinner that started with homemade soup.

We finished the meal about 7 p.m. It was too early to call it a night. I looked around the long, narrow table Sue and I shared with six other pilgrims, including Gert, Henrik, Vicky and Tom. Also at our table were Paul, a lanky Frenchman who stood about six-four and appeared to be about 70, and Charlotte, a cheerful woman from Holland 20 years younger.

A deck of cards beckoned from a game table next to the window.

A card game came to my mind. "Has anyone played Sorry, Charlie?"

Negative.

"Wanna play?"

Unanimous smiles and nods.

My poker group in Mariposa had played the game for years. It was always the last game of the evening, and one I could win, since it was mostly based on chance.

Each player starts with three chips and is dealt one card. The player with the lowest-value card after each round loses a chip. Play moves clockwise as each player keeps his or her card or trades it with the person to the left. That person repeats the process, and the game makes its way around the circle. Even I can figure out that I should trade a two, but keep a queen, when it is my turn. Now the fun part: kings. A player holding a king can block an attempted trade by flashing the king and saying, "Sorry, Charlie!" My Mariposa friends say, "Sorry, Charlie" in a mean, sarcastic tone that leads to wild fist and beer fights. Not really. The fights, I mean. Sarcasm? Let it roll! At the end of each round, old cards are discarded, and new cards are dealt. The last player still holding a chip wins the pot.

I explained the rules and gave examples. Charlotte translated for Paul. I surveyed the table. Eight pilgrims, four nationalities, aged teen to 70s. All looked like they were awaiting the first gift of Christmas.

Sue dealt the first hand, and I was left with a three, the lowest card of the round. I slid one of my chips to the middle of the table. No kings and no "Sorry, Charlie" during round one. The second time around the table, when it was Henrik's turn, he slid a card face down across to Paul the Frenchman, who scrunched up his long, narrow face and held his chin in his left hand. Paul had been quiet during dinner, and I had him pegged as a serious, even humorless person. Five, ten seconds ticked by. I wondered if Paul was confused about the rules. Around the table, anxious eyes awaited.

Paul suddenly broke into a super-sized grin and thrust both arms into the air.

"Ssssoooorrrreeee, Charlie!" he proclaimed in his French accent as he mockingly flashed his king at Henrik.

No group of pilgrims laughed as hard that night. The Dutch woman won the game, but it didn't matter. We had the time of our lives. I think St. James himself would have had a blast. For one Camino evening, it was the king of games, and a Frenchman stole the crown.

Several days later in a bustling village, I spotted Charlotte, the Sorry, Charlie champion, across the street, but couldn't remember her name.

"Sorry, Charlie!" I yelled, startling innocent bystanders.

She whipped around, grinned as wide as possible and waved.

I passed Paul twice during the next few days. Instead of the polite "Bonjour," we each said, "Sorry, Charlie!" and laughed.

Our stay in Rabé de las Calzadas was extraordinary. During breakfast at the Sorry, Charlie table, our host brought stacks of thick, fresh toast, and I covered several pieces with butter and homemade jam. I laughed to myself when I replayed Paul's smile the night before as he said the two magic words that would bond us forever.

I had taken a chance by offering the game, a risk I normally would have avoided with a group of mostly strangers. The game could have fallen flat, but I had planted the seed and then let the group do the rest, and they took the game beyond my expectations. I reached out and refrained from controlling the outcome. Finally, I went to bed in a communal dorm room and slept peacefully. At home, my usual bedtime routine after a social outing was to review what went wrong or mull over something stupid I said, and beat myself up.

As I basked in the tranquil morning, I told myself to hold the experience close. I was the son of a man who rarely connected with anyone, even his own family. I had struggled for years to resist my tendency to be like him. But one night, in a quiet Spanish village on the path of a revered pilgrimage, I had discovered a world of possibilities when I took a risk.

16

But My Wife Is in There

I climbed the stairs to our second-floor apartment, relieved that my cross-country coach had given my team a rare day off. I was the first one home and stopped at my tropical fish tank, turned on its light, and sprinkled TetraMin flakes on the water's surface. As usual, the angelfish was first to gobble before other, less aggressive fish, got their chance to eat.

There was a knock at the back door, which had a large window so I could see our neighbor, Derek, who held a basketball under his arm.

"Hey, Reg, how about some hoops?" He tossed the ball from one hand to the other. Derek had just moved in next door with his wife. They were in their thirties, and I had helped carry boxes up to their place when they moved in.

Basketball was definitely not my thing, but Derek had told me on move-in day that I looked like a natural. At 14, I was nearly six feet tall, but weighed a scant 120 pounds.

"You'll beef up in the next few years," Derek had promised.

"But I am terrible at sports. I am the slowest on my cross-country team."

"Well, maybe we can go to the school down the street someday and shoot around. No pressure."

Someday had arrived as Derek and I walked to the blacktop courts that featured chain nets hanging from rusty rims. Over the next few months, Derek patiently taught me how to shoot, dribble, and pass. I was flabbergasted at how quickly I improved and we were soon joining pickup games. Derek declined to accept the credit.

“Like I said, Reg, you’re a natural.”

I thought it was Derek who was the natural—at basketball and coaching—but I saw a great deal more in him. One Saturday morning as we walked to the school, he was curious about my family.

"What does your dad do?”

I was ready with my usual lie, hoping that Derek would never discover the truth. "He's a stock broker.”

"Wow, I never would have guessed. How do you like Oxnard High?”

"It's okay." Another lie. I sensed I could trust Derek, but part of me was afraid he would tell Mom if I told him the truth. I had shielded her from the extent of the bullying over the previous four years marked by more school changes than I care to remember. I was afraid she would go to the principal, and I knew that would make things worse.

"You're a good guy, Reg. I bet you have lots of friends at school.”

I looked at Derek and smiled as sincerely as I could. As we arrived at the courts, he changed the subject.

"Let's work on free throws today.”

I watched Derek bounce the ball three times before his free throw, a routine he said helped establish rhythm for the shot. As I did every day we were together, I dreamed that I had been born his son.

Just weeks after my rope-climb debacle, my PE class took up basketball. As we divided into teams, I was chosen last, as usual. The first day, I never touched the ball as my teammates avoided passing to me. But on the second day, a deflected pass put the ball in my hands on the baseline, about 15 feet out. I jumped, took a shot, flicking my wrist on my follow through just as Derek had taught me over and over. Swish.

“Spittle! Where did that come from?” one classmate yelled, shaking his head.

My shots didn't always go in, and I was still clumsy at times, but I gradually became a decent basketball player. It didn't stop jerks in the halls from saying, "Spittle" by spitting a loogie at my shoes, followed by "tull" when they passed me. But when basketball was the lesson plan, PE was no longer the darkest corner of my school day. Derek and I continued to play a couple of times a week until he and his wife moved away near the end of my freshman year. He and cross-country runner Jake had delivered comfort—and much more—during my first year of high school, just when I craved it most.

I had come to Spain burdened with baggage filled with insecurities. Like Derek and Jake, Gitta, James, and several others had been role models as I learned how to be a pilgrim on a great cross-country trek. They welcomed me to a world without the harsh judgments of the school hallways. So far, I had overcome physical hardships and had labored to distance myself from emotional shadows that had followed me for years. But I knew many more tests awaited.

We were officially traversing the meseta, the maligned and most skipped section of the Camino. The path crossed the northern part of Spain's 81,000-square-mile plateau that rose to more than 3,000 feet. Trekkers have often complained about the summer heat as well as the lack of shade, facilities, and water refill stations. Some clipped small umbrellas to their packs.

Our timing was perfect. The fields burst with late April green under warm sunshine as we walked with a rising sun and a gentle wind at our backs. No umbrella needed. The new grain bent in the breeze. We stretched eleven miles into a full day, with longer-than-usual breaks and a trailside picnic. At the edge of a broad, treeless hill, our gaze traveled more than 300 feet below to our destination, Hontanas. I imagined myself on horseback, surveying a Wild West town below. The domed church tower dominated the village, whose 70 inhabitants depended on up to 154 invaders who slept in its five albergues each night. The green slopes surrounding Hontanas would be brown in just a month or two.

Piles of rocks as tall as me lined parts of the meseta trail, and even higher stone walls defined our path into Hontanas. Sue and I ambled into the small village plaza that fronted the church. We had carried our packs 137 miles in 11 days as we stopped at El Puntido, the albergue across from the church. It had the usual bar furniture outside: dark green plastic tables and chairs along with green-and-white umbrellas.

Hontanas was like other small villages that were Spanish versions of American frontier outposts. I imagined wood siding and roof shingles instead of stucco, stone and tiles. Rather than cowboys, wearing chaps, riding through the dusty streets on horseback, Spain hosted sweaty, backpack-laden pilgrims hoofing along on cobblestones. The substitutes for shoot 'em up saloons were the omnipresent bars serving shots of espresso. Like Wild West towns, Camino villages attracted adventurers. Unlike towns on the American frontier, strangers were welcome, but they paid more than two bits for a whiskey. Luckily, walkers didn't pack rifles and pistols, or there might have been gunfights over snoring.

Inside El Puntido, a dark room housed a curved bar with stools awaiting happy hour drinkers. Down the hall, at the front desk, a woman in her late twenties with a low voice greeted, "Hola! How can I help you?" the Camino version of "Howdy, partner." Like so many other Spanish proprietors, she did everything she could to make us feel welcome.

We landed a third-floor room for €25 and added our names to the €10 pilgrim dinner list. Our host's question stopped us as we approached the stairs.

"Would you like us to do your laundry? Six euro per bag."

My answer came quickly. "That would be wonderful!"

On our way upstairs, we passed a dormitory packed with mostly young male trekkers who relaxed on their bunk beds. I was relieved I would not spend the night in that room. James, Gert, and Gitta would have marched right into the dorm and made themselves comfortable. I knew I could do that, but given a choice, I still opted for a room for just the two of us.

I unlocked the door to our room. Sue liked it immediately.

"This is so cute."

Dark wooden beams and panels covered a steeply sloped ceiling. White bedspreads adorned the twin beds that were common features in albergue private rooms. Thick towels were stacked at the foot of the bed. It had the charm of a room above a saloon without the red-and-white plaid curtains.

The communal shower room behind an unmarked door was not as charming. I discovered two small shower stalls behind doors of cloudy glass that would not conceal anyone in a game of hide-and-seek. Worse, there was no lock on the main door. If someone came in, he or she (or they?) might see me—naked! Heavens! I needed a shower in the worst way, so there was no option, really. I screwed up my courage, stripped in record time, and showered with my fingers crossed that I would preserve my hiding streak. I escaped unscathed, but when Sue was taking her shower, I watched the bathroom door like a hawk from our room as a man in his twenties approached, towel and toiletry bag in hand.

I had to stop him. "Sorry, but my wife is in there!"

He screeched to a halt, looked at me like I had said the craziest thing he had ever heard, and withdrew to the dorm room.

Later, I shared my guard-duty story with Sue, who was not impressed.

"I can take care of myself!"

The more I considered my impulsive action, the sillier I felt. At home, I probably would have lost sleep over my stupidity, like when I ruminated for weeks (months?) about my frozen pasta blunder. But in Spain, it became another lesson, and I was not embarrassed when I saw the guy a little later. He snapped a bath towel at my butt, though. Not really, but I wanted to put the lesson in a bottle and pack it back to California.

A tour of the dusty town revealed no sign of any Sorry, Charlie players from the night before. Like other towns we had seen, most of the albergues had been newly renovated with the yellow-orange stone-block walls and tiled roofs. Trekkers may object to the growing crowds on the Camino, but their euros have brought new opportunities for thousands of Spaniards.

The reflection of the late afternoon sun warmed the tiny plaza outside our albergue's bar, where I bought a beer for myself and a lemonade for Sue. We settled into chairs at a table outside.

Hontanas was 19 miles and a world away from Burgos. It was as quiet as Burgos was bustling. No families out for a stroll, no gift shops, no tapas bars. And nobody we knew, a rarity on the trek so far. After two days' rest in Burgos, we welcomed back the simplicity of the Camino.

My routine included cold lager after a day on the trail. I gulped a satisfying mouthful and watched three men with short, gray beards emerge from the bar carrying pints of beer. Wearing t-shirts, shorts, and sandals, they walked across the plaza and back after finding no place to sit.

"You are welcome to sit here," I said, pointing at the empty chairs at our table.

"Cheers," said the tallest of the three, and he jumped at the chance to sit. He was at least six-four, sported movie-star good looks, and smiled warmly as he reached out to shake my hand. Jack introduced his buddies Liam, the shortest of the three, and Daniel, a six-footer. As I was trying to figure out whether they were from Australia or New Zealand, Sue asked, "Where are you from?"

"Straya!"

I had not had enough beer to respond, "G'day!"

Jack told us he had planned to walk by himself when, just three weeks before his departure, Liam and Daniel, his friends of 40 years, approached him with a question:

"Can we come along?"

They were work mates, oil engineers whose jobs regularly took them around the world.

Daniel described their anticipated ending. "Our wives are meeting us in Santiago."

Liam said they had been staying in dorms since their start in St. Jean, France. They had even braved an albergue run by nuns where no alcohol was allowed.

"It was hell," Jack recalled as he glanced at his two friends. "But the nuns were wonderful to us otherwise."

"And Liam and I are sorry we asked Jack if we could come," Daniel said, straight-faced.

I was almost afraid to ask. "Why's that?"

"He snores like a hound!"

"On that note, it's time for another round of beers." I excused myself and hustled off to the bar. As the bartender filled a pitcher, I thought about the Australians. I had risked rejection in reaching out to them and felt more than just acceptance. Maybe I didn't look like such a pansy after all. More likely, they wanted to sit next to my pretty wife.

After another beer and conversation with the Australians, we reported to the dining room. I never would have predicted that dinner at the remote outpost would feel like we were on a cruise, but without the fine linen, silver, and name tags. However, it would include two desserts.

"We have you seated over here, Mr. and Mrs. Spittle," directed the woman who had checked us in a couple of hours before. Assigned seating was a curious pilgrim meal policy. I would have worn my clean t-shirt if I had known.

We were seated at a table for four with an attractive couple slightly younger than us. After introductions, Sue opened with a common conversation starter.

"What made you decide to walk the Camino?"

Sylvia and Stan glanced at each other, then looked down for a moment. Sue had "uh-oh" written on her face.

Sylvia got right to the point. "We're trying to save our marriage."

Stan saved us from having to follow that answer.

"The kids and grandkids are rooting for us back in Canada."

His wife continued.

"So far, so good."

Stan sent me an amused expression. The starters arrived and, as Sue and Sylvia talked, Stan asked what drew me to the Camino.

I briefly closed my eyes and saw Ron.

"The end of a close friend's life was the clincher, really. Sue had been pleading with me to walk the Camino, but I wouldn't commit."

"I know exactly what you mean, Reg. Life can change in an instant."

"So true." I leaned forward and rested my chin on my right hand as my elbow leaned on the table's edge.

I wanted to say more, but held back. I figured he would not want to hear about my personal struggles, but I contemplated my hope that I could transport the relatively carefree life and camaraderie home. Stan and Sylvia were trying to save their marriage, and I had a chance to remake the rest of my life.

I knew one subject I would not bring up with Stan and Sylvia. It was my parents' separation, another event from my consequential first year of high school. After we moved from the trailer to the apartment, Dad became so remote that my tropical fish seemed more accessible to me than my own father. As Derek, my neighbor, came into my life, my father left. Mom told me she couldn't take it anymore and had told Dad to leave.

I didn't think my much-older siblings Roy and Muriel knew what they were in for when Dad set off for Canada. During my two years in junior high school, what little respect I had for him had disappeared along with whatever passion he had for life. At the time, he was no longer a mystery man because I stopped caring why he was the way he was. I resented the man who took Mom for granted and pushed me farther away. As he followed the airport taxi driver, who carried Dad's luggage, down the stairs, I was never so relieved to see my father's back. Mom closed the door and breathed a deep sigh. The apartment finally felt like my home.

While I talked with Stan, I became convinced his kids were lucky to have him as a father. I hoped the Camino would send him and his wife home with a new marriage.

The four of us were eating our fresh-fruit desserts when the server entered the dining room carrying a tray full of caramel-covered flan. I faked a reach for one as she passed our table. "Ah, those look delicious." She shook her head, but smiled.

"Boy, did we order the wrong thing!"

The words were barely out of Sue's mouth when the server returned, placing a flan in front of each of us.

"Free samples. I hope you like it. Buen Camino."

Stan jumped out of his chair and gave the server a big hug. Well, not exactly. But his enthusiastic "*muchas gracias*" was likely more appropriate.

Before climbing into bed, I turned to my ritual repacking for a quick getaway in the morning. I unburdened my backpack of my REI mug and pillow. I had only used the cup once and my rolled up jacket would become my pillow when our accommodation did not supply one. The mug and pillow would find a new backpack if I left them in the room. For me, it would be less to pack, less to carry.

17

It's Just Five More Miles

El Puntido was one of my favorite albergues, and my review was sealed at breakfast by the delicious *tortilla de patata,* the Spanish egg and potato pie. If Denny's restaurants would add the dish to their menu, I would gladly take advantage of their senior discount.

The bartender who served us breakfast also taught me a coffee lesson that made my mornings more satisfying the rest of the way. For two weeks I had ordered a *cafe con pequeno leche*. I wanted strong coffee with a little cream or milk, but most of the time I got too much milk. He was among the few who had spoken English to me so far.

"Have you tried ordering an Americano?"

"Are they served in Spain?"

"Yes, and you could order hot milk on the side. Just say, '*leche caliente en el lado*.'"

His advice was one of several kindnesses offered by El Puntido staff. The people who own and run businesses are critical to the Camino. Also, volunteers from around the world come to Spain to work in albergues, making beds, cleaning bathrooms and otherwise making the journey as comfortable as possible. Thousands of people in hundreds of villages have opened their arms to pilgrims for centuries. Their Herculean effort matches the task.

Just three easy miles from El Puntido, a stone archway massive enough to fit a modern tour bus spanned the track amidst the ruins at San Antón. The Antonine Order, of French origin, established a monastery on the site of the impressive St. Anthony arch, which once supported a tunnel. We paused for photos before pointing our shoes toward another village perched below a mountain topped by castle ruins more than a thousand years old. Like many Camino villages, Castrojeriz is a narrow town built along the path. Most of the stone and stucco buildings had been restored, and several stores lined a covered sidewalk.

Castrojeriz is home to nearly 800 people, but it took only one resident to make a lasting impression in a way I could never have foreseen. Our main street stroll was interrupted by a short, grandfatherly type man in his 70s, wearing a bright green sweater. He was one of hundreds of Spaniards who had greeted us with "Buen Camino," but he was the only one who took a shine to Sue, kissed her on both cheeks and locked arms with her at the elbows.

He rattled off a string of sentences in Spanish.

"*No comprendo*," (I don't understand) she responded politely.

There was still more one-sided Spanish, with animation.

"*No comprendo*." A little louder, but still a friendly tone.

As the cute couple posed for my memorable photo, he continued his monologue. I believed he was just being friendly, and I did not detect that Sue was bothered. His voice drifted into the background as I explored the other end of the street, hoping Sue would stop being so polite. I was ready for lunch and had lost patience with his rambling.

I turned around, and Sue was marching quickly toward me. At first, she looked cross, but soon smiled as I eyed her questioningly.

"You left me. I had to let him kiss me—on the lips—to get away!"

Because of his age and cuteness factor, I had dismissed him as harmless. I am not sure what I would have done if I had stayed, and he kissed her in front of me, but I assume my hulking presence would have deterred his advance.

Noon approached as we exited town and studied the climb to Alto de Mostelares, at 2,952 feet. It was only about 400 feet of climbing, but there was no escape from the baking sun. The wide trail seemed to stretch forever up the side of the mountain. At the top, exhausted and sweaty, we took off our shoes and smelly socks (mine were, at least) and sat on a short stone wall at a rest area with a view back toward Castrojeriz. Somewhere in the town below, an old Spaniard wearing a green sweater was falling in love once again, but I knew the prettiest pilgrim had escaped. A breeze accompanied lunch, and we watched others labor up the path. The temperature was in the 80s, felt like the 90s, and it was April 24.

Perched at the edge of a plateau about a mile beyond our lunch stop, we spotted Itero de la Vega across the Rio Pisuerga at the bottom of a steep descent that mirrored our climb from Castrojeriz. We could make it an early day in Itero or hike five more miles to Boadilla del Camino.

I held the guidebook. "The albergue in Boadilla sounds better than anything in Itero." The description included "landscaped grounds with small swimming pool" and "family work tirelessly to offer the pilgrim a wonderful welcome." Two days' rest followed by two short days had left us feeling strong, but it was the only albergue in Boadilla, so we didn't want to take a chance on it being full. Minutes later, my phone call had put our name on a private room at En El Camino in Boadilla.

Passing through Itero de la Vega, we were buoyed by a brief reunion with Stan and Sylvia, the saving-their-marriage Canadians, who sat outside the 20-bed albergue they had wisely chosen. Itero was made up of just a few buildings, including three small albergues, in the middle of a flat plain.

"It's just five more miles," I pointed out when Sylvia warned about the rising temperature.

"I think there are beds here," she offered. I was tempted to join them in the cool shade of their covered walkway, especially when I spotted the two beers on their table.

"I'm sure we'll be fine, but thanks." I didn't say that I anticipated a room to ourselves.

We had forgotten about the consequences the first time we added five miles on a hot cinder surface onto a long day. I would have welcomed a camel to take us the rest of the way. I wondered where the water came from for the newly planted rows of farmland next to the path. Sue had to stop, air out, and rewrap her feet twice.

"I'm almost out of gauze and tape again." I flinched at Sue's words.

Three painstaking hours after Itero, we limped into Boadilla. The village of 140, like many on the trail, had been a thriving town of 2,000 that served a pilgrim hospital in medieval times. The re-awakening of the Camino brought new life to the outposts, but in Boadilla's case it was going to take time as the buildings we passed were crumbled, lifeless remains from better times. The first sign of life was a tall youthful trekker who warned as he passed, "The albergue is full. I think I got the last bed."

I was tempted to put my thumbs in my ears and flap my hands at him.

"We have a reservation."

"Lucky for you!"

I entered the albergue courtyard, a resort-like oasis with a swimming pool, lush lawn, and metal pilgrim sculpture. The three Australian engineers laughed in the shade of a large umbrella with tall beers on their table. I waved and expected a sympathetic, "Here, I saved this cold one for you, Reg!" All I heard was, "Hello, mate."

The next words were less welcoming.

"Another couple just checked into our last room," said the curly haired man at the registration desk.

"But I reserved a room hours ago! Don't you have our name written down?" I was nearly yelling.

He double-checked his register.

"Oh, here it is. I am sorry, but I gave the room to another American couple who said it was their reservation."

I was tired, frustrated. I sighed at the idea of trudging three more miles to Frómista. Common sense told me it would do no good to get angry.

"I am sorry I snapped at you. It has been a long day, but that's no excuse."

I looked at Sue and wondered how we could do another hour-plus of walking in the scorching afternoon after we had already logged 17 miles. And then the host held up his hand.

"Please, wait here. I will check with my brother."

He returned a few minutes later wearing a smile.

"We have a few beds upstairs."

We nearly cried in relief when we found our beds in a pleasant dorm room with six bunks. Two women, the only other occupants, offered friendly welcomes from their lower beds as we got settled. The bathroom had showers with such tight quarters that there was barely room to get undressed, but I didn't care. Beer, food, and gratitude topped my agenda.

Empty but brimming with anticipation, my stomach drew me into the large dining room. Nearly 50 trekkers joined Sue and me, seated around three long tables. Mouth-watering smells wafted from the kitchen as we joined a table with the three Australians, plus couples from Michigan and Berkeley, California. I sat across from three young eastern Europeans. I relished pilgrim meals in albergues, where people of all ages and nationalities had adventure on their minds and warmth in their hearts. After an outstanding meal of lentil soup, salad, pot roast and flan, the room erupted in cheers and applause when the chef, a matronly woman everyone called "Mama," came into the room. Bed, dinner, and breakfast had cost just €20 a person, including wine. A satisfying toast and eggs breakfast made it one of our favorite stops, despite the lost reservation and the overworked bathroom.

Twelve days of walking had taken us 154 miles, punctuated by 17 miles on our twelfth day that left us sore, tired and—despite the good breakfast—not in the best of spirits for day 13. Sue lacked enough tape and gauze to properly wrap her toes and was frustrated as we left the albergue.

We had barely hiked a quarter mile when I heard trekking poles hit the ground behind me.

"I can't do this!"

The Camino's magic act had fallen flat, but I had seen Sue overcome trying situations many times.

"It's just three miles to Frómista." I tried to be encouraging, but I knew not to go too far. "We can find a pharmacy and a place for second coffee." As sore as we were, our discomfort paled compared to medieval times when some pilgrims traveled barefoot and from farther afield. I understood why there had been so many hospitals along the pathway. We had it easy. The day was shaping up to be a formidable challenge, though.

Frómista was just what we needed. A pharmacy visit gave Sue all she required to dress her feet, which she said felt better afterward. Coffee and croissants completed the boost to our spirits.

A roadblock stopped us on the path through Frómista as a middle-aged shepherd and his flock of 200 crossed the Camino. The man stood like a school crossing guard on the street, but with a tall staff instead of a stop sign. The obedient sheep traveled toward a lush green field, directed by a dutiful sheep dog.

"Buen Camino!" The shepherd greeted us and waved before he followed his flock.

The Camino magic was returning to life, but its powers were limited. We soon discovered we had missed *our* shepherd—a yellow arrow—a few blocks back.

It was another sunny, warm day, but the 12 miles from Frómista to Carrión de los Condes were mostly pancake-like as the path bordered a busy two-lane highway. The packed-gravel trail was wide enough for a foursome to walk shoulder to shoulder. Flat concrete markers about waist high stood like gravestones and were imbedded with blue-and-gold scallop shells that marked the way toward the treeless horizon. It was the least picturesque day of our trek so far, but it would take us to a rest day so Sue could follow the hospital doctor's advice and get her foot checked at a local clinic.

Our steps to Carrión, a town of 2,300 that had 14 hospitals in medieval times, led us along a large plaza and past several bars and restaurants as we hunted for a place for two nights. Many albergues discourage or even prohibit multi-night stays as they clear out during the day for cleaning. We decided to splurge, so we found an en suite room at the Hostal Albe for €40 a night.

While we checked in at the hotel, a woman grabbed a huge suitcase in the lobby and waited behind us.

"Ah, a day-packer," I assumed. She had to be at least 50.

"Day-packer" was a sarcastic term reserved for trekkers who had their luggage shipped ahead each day. They carried a small pack and water. Travel companies booked the entire trip for them, including baggage transfer. Some rode buses to link the favored sections that they walked.

What had happened to the charitable "Do it your way" attitude that assumed there was no wrong way to hike the Camino? It still existed, most of the time. I did not hear many admit it, but there was a pecking order and "day-packer" was not first. Those who always stayed in dorm rooms in the cheapest albergues, cooked their own food and carried only the barest necessities, rated much higher. That put us somewhere in the middle. We also used Wi-Fi (pronounced wee-fee in Spain) and iPads to blog every day, both no-nos to purists. I suppose we should all have gone bare foot and lived off the land. But I did not find that the Camino was home to strong cliques. There was some light-hearted gaming, but rarely to the point of exclusion.

We exchanged greetings with day-packer Cynthia, who was English, in the hotel lobby and found her distant and negative about the experience.

"It isn't very difficult, is it?" she asked. "I did 18 miles the other day."

"Did you carry a backpack?" Sue asked.

"No." Enough said. She didn't look like she could carry half of what was in her suitcase, and I wondered how she was going to get it up to her room.

After we freshened up, we wandered through the winding cobblestone streets to a bar with tables outside for happy hour. Like many bars, it bordered the Camino path. Minutes later, Emily and Hannah (the Americans celebrating their 60th birthdays enjoying their first meet-up since high school) approached, still wearing their packs.

As I hugged Emily, I remembered her shouted expletive at the four early risers the week before.

"We're having a great time. Hannah took a bus a couple of times, but we rendezvoused within a day."

We bought them drinks, then they continued their day. It would be the last time we would see Emily and Hannah. Although we had spent just hours together, they felt like good friends.

My grumbling stomach told me it was dinner time.

"Do we have to eat again?" Sue smiled.

A sign advertised "pilgrim meal" for €12 outside a bar, and we were drawn inside by the laughter that traveled through the door. We sat at the bar for our second round of drinks. A man and woman in their early twenties slouched, legs outstretched, at the table behind us. I overheard him talking about a blog he was writing, so I swiveled around to ask him about it.

"I am writing about walking the Camino. My family is following me." He explained he had taken time off from his job back home in New Mexico, but had bad news.

"I have shin splints," a common trekking complaint.

The bar door opened, and there was Cynthia, who slid onto a barstool next to Sue. The shin-splint man moved chairs to make room around his table. "You are all welcome to join us; we are having dinner too."

"I just love the Camino, don't you?" Cynthia had changed her tune since our hotel lobby talk.

After introductions, Cynthia countered my expectations again. "I would love to hear everyone's favorite Camino experience."

After several testimonials, Cynthia said that the evening with us was one of her best experiences so far.

"I love meeting people from other countries."

"You would enjoy the albergue pilgrim meals," Sue suggested.

"I'm booked in hotels the entire way, but I hope I can find more trekkers like you in the bars."

We were on dessert by the time we finished our stories. Cynthia's story starter was perfect. Our first impression of the English trekker had been off target. Once again: Never assume.

The next morning, we found the medical clinic at the other end of town, where Sue, with no appointment, waited just half an hour before two doctors examined her foot in a small room. The redness was gone, and "it is healing well," one doctor said. "Take the rest of the antibiotics and you should be fine." The visit cost €60, and our travel insurance reimbursed us. Spain's health care system was two-for-two.

Before leaving Carrión, we checked our progress. Realistically, would we be able to finish? We had about three weeks before our return flight from Madrid. There were 257 miles left, about 90 on the meseta. Allowing for at least two days in Santiago and a day to get to Madrid, we would have to average more than 14 miles a day if we didn't take any more rest days. Were we tempting fate by hiking on the hot meseta surface? We had seen young people go home due to injuries, mostly foot-related. And we were no strangers to foot problems. Our goal of completing the entire trek was already compromised by starting in Pamplona and the 15-mile taxi ride to Burgos.

We got up early the next morning and walked—to the Carrión bus station, where we waited for our ride to León.

Standing on the sidewalk outside the station, our eyes met.

I struggled to come to terms with our shortcut. "Remember when we vowed to finish all 500 miles?"

"But I don't feel like we've failed. We haven't gone every mile, but think of all the experiences we have had. We have done really well, honey. If I'm going to skip part, I would rather it be the meseta than Galicia."

I surveyed the flat, hot, shadeless Camino from the air-conditioned bus during most of the 60 miles. I felt no joy in the compromise. I was glad the sweaty trekkers who braved the trail could not see through the dark windows to the cheaters on the bus. As we sped by, guilt weighed on me, but I knew we had made the right choice.

In just more than an hour, we had saved five days of walking in the hot sun.

Nearing León, I felt a wealth of anticipation for the remaining 197 miles.

18

A Fantastic Moment

It felt like Scotty had beamed us to another world when our bus pulled into León. A modern city of 127,000, it didn't fit with the Spain we knew. For just €35, we rented a large room with a shared bath at the Pensión Sandoval. As we frittered away the afternoon on streets lined with tourist sites, bars, shops, and restaurants, I couldn't shake my uneasy feeling. Something about the metropolis didn't feel right.

For the moment, León offered what we needed to continue our Camino: new pilgrim passports. Ours were full of stamps from bars, albergues, and even random places where people inked their unique seal. We found a large Catholic albergue and climbed the narrow stairs to the office, where a short, wiry, gray-haired church official sat at a reception table. He was happy to give us passports for a €2 donation. He handed me mine after methodically scripting my name and US passport number on the inside cover.

A 13th century gothic cathedral is the city's most spectacular building. Constructed on the former site of Roman baths and later a royal palace, it is nicknamed the House of Light. I focused on the powerful towers outlined sharply by the brilliant blue sky. Once inside, I gawked at the legendary stained glass, which measured 19,300 square feet and brought a kaleidoscope of light into the cavernous church. So far, I had toured two of the three great cathedrals of the Camino de Santiago: León and Burgos. The greatest one waited 197 miles away—about 400,000 steps—in Santiago.

In search of refreshments, we returned to the downtown streets where we had passed bars and restaurants. That part of the city was modern and fast-paced, with cars, buses, and crowds. We found a tiny table in a glitzy bar filled with young people and loud pop music. If there were any other pilgrims in the bar, they were disguised as part of the Saturday date night crowd.

But as Sue and I raised our glasses of chardonnay for a toast, I realized what had been nagging me most of the afternoon: I had been transported back into the future. The modern city, with its honking horns, bright lights, and clothing fashion statements filled me with longing for the sweaty t-shirts, smelly shoes, and simpler Camino life I had come to love. The bus trip left me feeling like I had committed a crime against the spirit of the pilgrimage, and I yearned for the peace of the real Camino.

As we departed León at 8 the next morning, the Saturday night celebrating was winding down and a bachelorette party was breaking up. The unsteady bride-to-be wore a white veil and the biggest penis hat I had ever seen. Two feet tall (but I didn't measure), with the tip pointing straight upward. It was plastic, and the detail appeared to be marginally realistic. I wanted to take a photo for our blog, but Sue forbid it. Too bad; I had already considered a few entertaining titles. We had seen the five women the evening before in the bar, hatless and visibly soberer.

The footpath led us across a huge plaza, and we quickly recognized the five-star hotel. It was the Parador Hostal San Marcos de León, where Tom (Martin Sheen) paid for luxurious rooms for his three Camino friends in the movie, thinking they would appreciate privacy after weeks in albergue dorms. That evening, Tom learned a lesson about the strong bonds of his Camino family when, one by one, they knocked on his door. None wanted to be alone after all. There are several other paradors on the Camino. Parador is a government-run business that turns historic castles, convents, monasteries, and other buildings into luxury hotels. The most famous is next to the cathedral in Santiago.

After five miles of tracing the Camino along León's streets, a familiar sight appeared at the edge of the city: Trekkers sat outside a bar, backpacks propped against the building. "Buen Camino!" they greeted. Our backpacks joined the others, and we found plastic chairs, coffee, and a second breakfast prepared and served by three generations of a family. We had not met our fellow pilgrims before, but I felt like they were welcoming us home.

After our breakfast party, the trail led us across a deserted highway and back onto the remaining stretch of the meseta. Nature called as our second coffee hit us on a lonely stretch between bars, our usual stops for toilets. We waited for a group of trekkers to pass before we relieved ourselves behind some bushes about the size of large tumbleweeds. Many packed small plastic bags for their used paper and covered their deposits like cats. An important lesson is to look before stepping, though.

I finished quickly, partly because my aim was better than Sue's, and returned to the trail in time to warn Sue that trekkers were approaching. Two attractive women about our age saw our backpacks on the ground and asked if we were all right.

"Er, we're fine, thanks." I wasn't sure why I felt embarrassed, but it was nice of them to ask.

The women barely slowed as they passed at near freeway speed. We breathed their dust on the mostly flat pathway wide enough for a farm tractor. The highlight was a picnic spot with a table and a view of the flat, green landscape. Several large shade trees broke up the skyline. An enterprising entrepreneur in his thirties sat in the shade of his car's tailgate, offering thirsty or hungry pilgrims an ice chest full of drinks and a small table topped by candy, chips, and fruit. We had passed a few of the impromptu snack bars along the way; some had no one tending them and depended on the honor system. I bought a Nestles chocolate bar that would propel us the remaining five miles to Villar de Mazarife.

We entered the village of 400 residents after a 14-mile day and were drawn to a modern trailside bungalow housing the first of three albergues, San Antonio de Pádua. At the end of most days, we were keen to unload our backpacks at our earliest chance, so the first albergue usually got our business. The San Antonio had an extra allure: A sign next to the entrance advertised Pepé Giner's cooking. Our hunger chose for us. A tiny, private room downstairs with a window next to the green grass, was ours for €30, including a large, shared bathroom with shower and toilet stalls. I was glad we avoided the crowded dorm room, filled with enough bunks for about 40. Our smartest decision was to book Pepé's meal for €10 each.

The town had character, including a church bell tower inhabited by storks and their big, messy nests. I watched one huge stork come in for a landing and quickly moved to stay out of its flight (and bombing) path. A corner bar across the cobblestone street appeared busy. Perfect. We pushed open the door and saw that it was packed with elderly Spanish men, sitting around tables, playing dominoes. Every eye remained focused on the tiles as we entered. It was a remarkable sight, and the atmosphere resembled a chess match. I was tempted to yell "Domino!" I glanced toward the bar across the room and recognized two people who didn't fit the bar's demographic.

Sue leaned toward my left ear. "Honey, there are the ladies from our potty stop."

They waved us over to the bar.

"You two walk fast," I said after meeting Judy, from Australia, and Verna, a Texan. The four of us sat at the bar, glasses of wine within reach. The bartender battled boredom by drumming his fingers on the counter; the domino players were not drinkers, and I was near certain the room served as a community center.

"This is our first day; we just started in León," Verna explained. "I hope I can keep up with Judy, but mostly I want to make it to Santiago in two weeks."

Judy and Verna wore something I had seen on few women (except for my wife) the last two weeks: earrings. They significantly raised the low bar for Camino fashion.

Sue went with the risky question. "So, what brought you here?"

"We grew up together in Texas and have been friends for 50 years," Verna said as she looked at Judy. "Judy met a doctor from Ecuador, and they moved to Australia in 2010 for Judy's job."

"We're turning 60 this year and wanted to celebrate with a reunion, so here we are." As Judy talked, I couldn't help thinking she appeared to be younger than 60.

Verna said they had a backup plan if they can't finish the nearly 200 miles to Santiago. "We'll head south and sit on the beach."

After witnessing their strength on the trail earlier, I doubted swim suits and sand were in their near future. I had another option.

"Or, you could hang out here and play dominoes."

Verna scanned the roomful of potential domino coaches. "What a wonderful idea!" She missed my Groucho Marx eyebrow impression.

Later, the four of us sat with other pilgrims at a long, narrow table in the albergue dining room as Pepé Giner prepared our vegetarian evening meal. We learned he was a physiotherapist, and I wondered if I should ask him to massage my aching shoulders. Seriously; if he had not also been the chef, I might have asked. Pepé worked busily in a large, well-equipped kitchen next to the dining room while 40 hungry adventurers waited.

On our Camino, talk usually came easily, like it did with Judy and Verna. Family and career histories seldom dominated, or even came up. Conversation was often light-hearted, but not always. Philosophical discussions sometimes went deep. Around the dinner table with Verna and Judy, there was some potty talk. Verna was using the women's bathroom upstairs to avoid the multi-sex facility near the private room she shared with Judy. I figured she would probably not be comfortable using a stall with a man in the next one. If she was like me, she would become more comfortable with the idea as her trek continued. I was relieved that I was not the only one who came to Spain with bathroom worries.

Pepé won an ovation for his delicious three-course pilgrim dinner and was up early the next day to cook me a special birthday breakfast. In reality, he had no idea it was my birthday, but he had fixed a tasty buffet anyway. I don't get worked up about my birthdays, but my mom sure used to. She cooked roast beef and Yorkshire pudding, my favorite dinner. She wore a cone-shaped birthday hat with a rubber-band strap under her chin when she brought my homemade chocolate cake with chocolate frosting while singing in her Irish accent. I have always missed Mom the most on my birthday and number 61 was no different in that sense. But it was so unfamiliar in other ways. I would celebrate by walking to a destination yet to be determined. I would sleep on a bed in a mystery Spanish village. I knew dinner wouldn't be roast beef and Yorkshire pudding; there would be no birthday cake either. As long as there was a bed, shower, and dinner. And Sue, the best part.

On my way out of the albergue, I committed my daily crime, theft of a wad of toilet paper from the bathroom for the road. It was still the meseta and the distance between bars tested our holding power. I briefly considered lifting a few things from the breakfast buffet for lunch as well, but I saw Pepé scrubbing dishes in the kitchen and couldn't bring myself to take extra food from such a hard-working man. I decided to stop at a store on the way out of town instead.

Temperatures had plunged overnight and rain was forecast on the last part of the meseta. At breakfast, a trekker had announced that snow was likely in the Galicia mountains beyond the meseta. We wore our rain gear, including a cover on our packs, as we rejoined the wide path out of Vilar de Mazarife. I was warm and dry in my rain jacket and rain pants in a light, windy drizzle. Just ahead a couple of middle-aged trekkers struggled to stay dry despite wearing ponchos. I wondered if they were going to become airborne like Mary Poppins as their super-wide coverings flapped wildly in the wind. I had heard people promote ponchos because they were lightweight and covered backpacks, but I was a rain jacket snob.

"What's that?" I wondered just minutes out of town, after the rain had paused. Someone behind us was singing and approaching so fast I wondered if she was a bicyclist.

I turned around in the middle of the song and was startled to see Judy, who was singing a birthday song in Spanish. It was a fantastic moment, and I will remember Judy's song every birthday the rest of my life. Hugs, then Judy and Verna darted ahead, leaving us wondering if they could keep up their roadrunner-like speed. They had to be walking considerably faster than three miles per hour. We probably averaged two-and-a-half, at best. The packs slowed us down, but our legs were much stronger than when we began. I overheard one skinny teen-ager brag how he was getting more muscular legs on the trek. I don't think mine changed visibly, unfortunately. Still a beanpole, but a stronger one.

Sue's blisters had steadily gotten better since our rest in Carrión. We were getting on with the Camino with a tinge of sadness about having to skip part of the meseta. It was the right thing to do, but still felt like cheating. Our new goal was to trek the remaining 183 miles to Santiago, matching how far we had walked so far.

After 12 miles, we began our hunt for accommodation, saving Astorga for the next day. We traversed the Puente de Orbigo, one of Spain's longest and most picturesque medieval bridges, to the small village of Hospital de Orbigo. The place was not particularly inviting from our view, so we decided to check out the next two villages; each had one albergue. It was a great call, as it turned out, but a risk I wouldn't have taken before the Camino.

Villares de Orbigo was just up the road. Swirling wind whipped along the deserted street. It had the feel of another frontier ghost town, and we were drawn to it. On the first building's orange stucco side wall, "albergue" was spelled out as part of a mural depicting laundry hanging on clotheslines. The front was yellow with orange trim and was freshly painted. The doorway opened to a brick-floored courtyard, revealing a construction project. Old stucco had been chipped away from one wall, exposing bricks. I was intrigued.

"What do you think, honey?"

"It is a little rough, but looks okay."

A handsome bearded Spaniard in his thirties emerged from a room.

"*Buenos dias.* Welcome!"

"Hola, do you have a room for tonight?" I asked.

"It would be my pleasure; would you like a tour first?"

Pablo said he was converting the former sheep barn into an albergue and had finished several rooms. He brimmed with pride as he showed us small dorm rooms upstairs and a downstairs room with two sets of bunks and a large, modern bathroom with a step-in shower. All had been freshly painted and were a bit stark, but comfortable. No sheep pellets anywhere. I was saddened when he informed us that he lost his building contracting business in Madrid when the economic downturn hit. He moved to Villares de Orbigo with his wife, whom he had met on the Camino, and their new baby.

"You have done beautiful work with your albergue, Pablo," I said when he stamped our passports.

As we debated which room to take, he made the decision easy when he told us the downstairs room was the only one so far that was heated. The room was €30, and, as it turned out, we had the albergue to ourselves.

"Could I offer you dinner and breakfast? It would be twelve euro per person."

Good fortune was my partner at Pablo's albergue. "That would be great."

Was it ever. A salad included lettuce, rice, crab, tuna, walnuts, and raisins. I even ate the tuna. Freshly baked bread accompanied a scrumptious vegetable-beef-lentil stew. A bottle of wine, dessert, and special birthday photo memory were icing on the cake. Pablo was the perfect host.

We departed Pablo's budding albergue after he served a ham-and-egg breakfast. I was surprised I felt so emotional when I waved as he stood in the courtyard with his wife, who held their baby. I felt like I was leaving an old friend and hoped that many other pilgrims would chance upon his hospitality.

19

Follow Me!

After three weeks in Spain, my focus had shifted to basic needs, not wants. I had discovered that modest expectations can ironically bring astonishing outcomes. I had found joy in simplicity.

But what if I faced a night without the basics, like no bed or food? On the last day of April, I would find out if the Camino would continue to provide.

A cold, drizzly morning marked our final day on the meseta, where the wide trail guided us over nine miles of green, rain-soaked rolling hills to Astorga, known as the gateway to the mountainous region of Galicia.

On our way, a curious, rustic outpost drew our gaze. A run-down cement block building the size of a single-wide manufactured home bordered the trail. Two trekkers huddled shoulder-to-shoulder on a bench, protected from the rain by a flimsy, narrow metal roof attached to the building. A man wearing a long, green poncho stood next to a small food cart. As we stepped over puddles, the man turned around, and I immediately recognized him.

"Gert!" I was excited to see our German friend, whom we had lost track of after the Sorry, Charlie game. I considered hugging him, but we were both drenched, and I was not sure he was a hugger. Instead, we exchanged fond greetings and a wet handshake.

Feet were the topic of conversation as Gert and Sue caught each other up on the latest. We were glad to hear Gert felt better. By necessity, virtually everyone was a podiatrist on the Camino. The amateur psychologist in me wondered what drew Gert to Spain by himself, but I resisted a question he might find too forward. He was friendly and occasionally made jokes, but I sensed a fellow introvert who may have been struggling with some ghosts of his own.

We walked together for a couple of miles, catching up on tales from the trail. Sue and I kept going while Gert took a break, understanding we would meet up later. We soon came to a ridiculously elaborate pedestrian bridge over the train tracks to Astorga. A series of switchbacks reached three stories above the ground. We turned around to marvel at the structure we had climbed and descended when, there he was again. We laughed while watching Gert crisscross on the bridge, carrying his large backpack, his poncho flapping in the wind.

The three of us entered market day in Astorga, population 12,000, as crowds of shoppers in a light rain negotiated stalls in the Plaza Mayor. A three-level church with a bell tower and two spires marked one end of the plaza. Juliet balconies watched from some of the three- and four-story medieval buildings.

Gert looked at the cafe ahead. “Should we have lunch here?”

“Sure, it’s not picnic weather.” I opened the glass door, revealing a noisy, crowded eatery with a roaring fireplace. We wormed our way to a small table and found a sliver of floor for our backpacks. It was packed with locals, who paid us little attention. *Peregrinos* (pilgrims) were a common sight. We ordered a table-full of hot food, ate every bite, and washed it down with steaming coffee.

Gert extended his stay in Astorga while Sue and I walked three miles to a fork in the road at Murias de Rechivaldo, a tiny Maragato village. The Maragatos are Moorish people linked to the Berbers of North Africa. About 4,000 live in the region around Astorga. We had a decision to make: Stay at one of three albergues in Murias, or detour to a place that Pablo, our host the previous night, had enthusiastically recommended. We found a description in our trusty Brierley guidebook:

"Castrillo de Polvazares (is a) traditional Maragato village with cobbled main street lined with stone buildings providing tourist rooms, bars and restaurants. Painstakingly rebuilt by local artisans it lacks the authentic ambience found in the crumbling villages spread along the Camino itself."

A mixed review, but should we take a chance? The guidebook noted there were two albergues, and it was just a mile and a half away. As we read, Gert caught up with us.

"Let's see what he thinks."

"Yes, I will go with you!"

The cold, damp weather tagged along as well. In less than an hour, we reached the cobbled main street. As advertised, the small village's stone buildings had been updated, and the few bars showed modest signs of life. However, our search for albergue beds came up empty, and we paused on the main street. We were tired, wet, desperate for a dry home for the night.

"There are three albergues in Santa Catalina," I said. "Or we go back."

"It's getting dark, and it's more than an hour to Santa Catalina." Sue's reality check had us shaking our heads. "Going back is a bit closer."

"Where's a taxi when we need one?" I asked.

I was about to suggest that we walk to the next town when an old, small pickup stopped next to us. A man with short, gray hair rolled down his window, stuck out his head and shouted questions in Spanish so fast that I had no clue what he said. Gert talked to the driver, also in Spanish, then turned to us with the bad news.

"He said both albergues here are not open for the season yet." We eyed each other quizzically, even panicked-looking. A wet journey in near darkness loomed. We could not be certain there would be empty beds in the next village.

Suddenly, the man put his truck in gear and yelled, "*Sígueme*!" (Follow me.)

He stopped about 50 yards away, jogged up some stairs and knocked on an apartment door. A matronly woman stuck out her head. Soon, our new Spanish friend descended the stairs holding a ring of keys. Now what? He led us a block away to a circular tower and a door that opened to a narrow, spiral staircase. At the top, there was our home for the night (for €4 each), a spartan room with seven mattresses on metal frames, but no bedding. A single light bulb hung from the middle of the ceiling. It was the municipal albergue, and he opened it just for us. Through interpreter Gert, he told us there would be no heat, but he would turn on the hot water so we could have showers in the two small bathrooms off the dorm room.

In just a few minutes, we progressed from homelessness to living in a bedroom with bathrooms (and hot showers). I felt like we had found the Ritz. And the Camino wasn't done for the day. After we cleaned up and rested while bundled up in the cold room, we ventured out to find dinner. We had hungrily spied people in several bars and restaurants on our way through town, so our appetites were ready.

Dumbfounded, we stood in the middle of an intersection. The streets were deserted, and every place was closed, except for one fancy restaurant. I peeked inside and realized that my trekking raincoat, t-shirt, wet boots and hiking pants were not going to be welcome. A coat and tie had not made it into my backpack. I closed the door and faced Gert and Sue with discouraged eyes.

"I have a couple of granola bars in my pack." It was not what they wanted to hear.

We wheeled around when we heard a familiar voice. It was the matronly woman at the top of the stairs with the keys, who shouted to us, "*Comida*?" (food) Before we could answer, she scrambled down the stairs and waved at us to follow her as she scurried along the street. She banged (knocked would not be accurate) on a restaurant door even though the sign in the window read, "*Cerrado*" (closed). The door opened just enough for her loud commands to enter, and moments later we were seated at a round table with a white tablecloth, fine silverware, wine glasses, the works. It was without a doubt the nicest restaurant of our Camino, and I was overwhelmed. I looked for our savior, but she had returned to her upstairs flat before we could give thanks.

Servers brought us water, superb red wine, a wonderful starter plate and a delicious garbanzo bean soup. I was startled by the next course: a large, oval plate piled high with cooked animal feet, ears, tongue, and unfamiliar round pieces. Gert got down to business quickly; Sue and I picked out a few chunks that looked like the meat we were used to eating. It was good, actually. The Camino provided, but not for free. It cost €20 a person, but it was priceless.

Soon we were back in the dorm room, bundled in our sleeping bags, wearing several layers, including down jackets. Then we saw it: our breath. It was that cold. But we were grateful to be out of the rain without the extra walk to the next village. We piggy-backed Wi-Fi on Gert's phone hotspot and checked e-mail, downloaded photos and read the news until his phone ran out of poop. By then we had too. I turned and lowered my iPad onto the floor, allowing freezing air to enter an opening in my warm sleeping bag. Shivers shot up my spine. I pulled back and scooted my head down into the bag. Warmth gradually returned.

As I waited for sleep, I chuckled to myself when I realized there was one Camino threat surely absent. We had been on semi-alert most nights, but had not encountered the bedroom vampires known as bed bugs. Some trekkers lived in terror of being attacked at night, but we had not seen any of the tiny critters and we thought they probably waited for warmer weather to swarm upon sleeping pilgrims. No doubt, it was too cold in our room. We would be in more danger in an expensive, warm hotel in California.

I had been asleep for a couple of hours when I felt a poke.

"Honey, turn over, you're snoring."

Later, Sue did it again. I had barely gotten back to sleep when I felt yet another jab in my back.

None of the nasal outbursts had come from me, though.

"It's not me! It's Gert."

We had a late-night laugh, but I was not about to poke him.

I peered out of my sleeping bag to see the early morning light as it penetrated the uncovered windows. My movement let a shaft of freezing air into my sleeping bag. I spied my rain jacket on the bathroom door, where I had hung it to dry. It was another layer of potential warmth. I jumped out of bed, put on my raincoat, found my gloves, and squirmed into my shoes. It was coffee time! I knew it was going to be a great morning despite the cold. I was grateful that packages of instant Starbucks coffee had come to Spain in my backpack. I descended the spiral staircase to the kitchen, where I found a kettle and started some water on the electric stove.

I was on a roll, ready to bet the limit. "Ah, the warm burner, I will turn them all on as well as the oven. Maybe we can huddle around some warmth with our coffee."

Maybe not. The sudden surge of power demand tripped something, and everything went dark and dead. Sue also lost her light in the windowless bathroom upstairs.

Gert, who had turned on the hot water in both showers in an attempt to warm the upstairs, tromped down in seconds. He quickly found the breaker, the stove surged back to life, and I made do with one burner.

As we stood next to the stove and sipped our steaming cups of coffee, I unfolded my pilgrim passport to see what the pickup driver had stamped when we checked in the night before. It showed a cloaked walker carrying a pack, gripping a tall staff, portraying millions who had returned home with their stories of Camino magic.

I hoped that I would remember the lessons from Castrillo. Allow others to help. Don't feel like I have to be the one to fix everything. Be patient. Gert, the pickup driver, the mystery woman as well as cooks and servers, had come through. The last 14 hours in Castrillo had been surreal. Somehow, we had found beds, a meal, and coffee. Just our basic needs, but they felt like a great deal more.

20

Why Don't You Love Me?

I hit bottom on the first day of May. I had slept little the night before in the cold albergue in Castrillo. I could blame Gert's snoring, but it wasn't that bad. I could blame the 1,700 feet of climbing, but that was not enough to merit complaint. My shoulders ached from carrying my backpack, but everyone worked through pain on the Camino. When we finally reached the freezing mountaintop village of Foncebadón at the end of the day, I threw down my pack and plopped down outside in a plastic chair, feeling disheartened. What had happened?

May 1 had begun in chilling fog with a one-hour uphill hike from our Castrillo detour back to the main trail. We embarked soon after the first morning light, and the landscape was like the vast expanse of chaparral in California. The Starbucks coffee was a great kickoff, but we eagerly anticipated breakfast after we rejoined the Camino.

"Gert, you saved us in Castrillo," I said as we followed a dirt road with grass growing between the tire tracks. "What would Sue and I have done without your Spanish and quick action with the electrical breaker?"

"I am glad you and Sue had coffee!" We were all freezing, but Gert exuded warmth with his usual graciousness.

Despite the hardships, I knew the past 14 hours had been remarkable.

"I am not sure how I would describe our detour, but I know one thing: I will never forget it."

Sue agreed. "A crazy adventure and a test for all of us."

"I think we passed," Gert decided. "But we had help, didn't we?"

Gert, Sue, and I were relieved to get out of the cold when we found a casual cafe in Santa Catalina. I opened the door to a warm room and stood with my arms wrapped around myself as I studied the menu posted behind the counter. Several pairs of trekkers sat with hot beverages and light breakfast fare.

We carried trays with our toast, juice, and coffee to a table in the back of the small dining room. I yearned for a plate of eggs and potatoes. Instead, I settled for a banana.

"Gert, what is the Spanish word for banana?"

"*Platano*, I think."

I returned to the counter. "*Un platano, por favor.*"

"Oh, you must want a banana," said the server in beautiful English. Giggles from Sue and Gert. So, I got my banana, and everyone in the place got a round of laughter. It turns out banana is a localized word in Spanish. In some places, a banana is a banana. But I awarded myself points for trying.

Gert sped ahead after breakfast while Sue and I took a more leisurely pace on a level three-mile section. We hoped the next village would have a bar with a bathroom. Public bathrooms were nearly non-existent, and we had learned to go when we were in a bar—whether we needed to or not—even if it meant buying a cup of coffee as payment.

The next town was El Ganso, which the guidebook called "a hauntingly crumbling village, evoking a sense of loss…" A pilgrim hospital and monastery operated here in the 12th century. The only sign of life as we entered town was the often-photographed Cowboy Bar. It was yet another outpost that had sprung up as Camino traffic surged. A narrow, stucco building, it had a thin, wooden door that was propped open under a wooden sign spelling "Cowboy" in capital letters. Another sign testified in Spanish that the bar was the best of the best. In El Ganso, it was the one and only. Sue and I shared a coffee and bladder relief at the otherwise empty bar.

Outside in the damp cold was another incongruous sight. Two bicyclists, dressed in gear that would be at home on the Tour de France, ate granola bars as they loitered next to their mountain bikes. Many parts of the walk would not be difficult on bikes, but the mountains offered special challenges: rocks, mud, and narrow sections. And trekkers. Most of the time, bicyclists rang a bell or shouted out before they passed. "Buen Camino" greetings were usually exchanged. But there were some close calls when they just zoomed by. One stealth biker bumped Sue on a steep, rocky, downhill grade, nearly knocking her over. The rider continued on without even a "Buen Camino."

The cold, relentless climb, and lack of sleep took their toll in the afternoon. As I struggled over a rocky section, I weighed my foul mood. I knew the toughest times were tests that could be transformative, but I was giving up. Moments later a trekker streaked past me and cheerfully threw a "Buen Camino!"

I muttered "Buen Camino," but really meant "Go to hell." My mood was beyond repair. Sue patiently waited at each turn for me to catch up.

The temperature dropped, and the incline steepened as we continued toward Foncebadón, another village littered with ruins. It had snowed in Foncebadón the night before, and we had seen the white dusting from the trail below hours ago, but it had melted by the time we finished our 13-mile day. Four stone-sided albergues rose from the crumbling remains of buildings.

I imagined a long, cold night on a mattress next to farting, snoring pilgrims. At the first albergue, I was so spent that I pitched my backpack to the ground and collapsed into a plastic chair.

"If I hear one more 'Buen Camino,' I'm going to scream!" I buried my face in my hands, my elbows on my knees.

Sue tapped me on the head as she passed on her way up the rock stairs leading to the hostel's reception room. "Please, let there be beds and heat," I fantasized as I shivered. Several trekkers passed as I sat.

"Buen Camino!" they greeted graciously, calling my bluff.

My face remained buried until Sue returned.

"Honey, we have a private room, with our own bath and heat!" Sue announced, dangling a key in front of me. I wasn't expecting much, but the second-floor room was deluxe. I was energized despite the fact that I had crumbled like the ruins that surrounded our accommodation. When the chips were down, the Camino provided. So did my wife.

Our albergue, the Convento de Foncebadón, featured a busy bar and a crowd of very happy customers. Yelling and loud laughter filled the room. At one bar a week earlier, a middle-aged Canadian trekker we had befriended confronted a table full of rowdy young people and reminded them they were on a pilgrimage. Fortunately, he had not been punched in the nose, and they honored his request to lower their voices. I don't think he would have been as successful at quieting the crowd in Foncebadón.

Noisy trekkers were commonplace in bars, rest stops, and albergues. Partying trekkers contrasted sharply with those who came to Spain for spiritual reasons and preferred quiet respect.

We exchanged the noisy bar for the quieter albergue dining room, where Gert had settled into a table while checking the news and weather on his phone. I groaned as I took a seat across from him. "That was a tough day."

"I have the perfect medicine for you, Reg." He crossed the room to the bar and returned moments later with a shot glass. "Spain's best liquor for you." It was just what I needed. I can't remember what it was, but it had a smooth taste with a kick. Gert had earned yet another "thoughtful pilgrim" award.

We enjoyed a restful, warm night in the town that mirrored an earthquake-induced disaster area. Castrillo, our detour town, was a neatly trimmed place that provided our least comfortable room of the Camino. Foncebadón, amongst the ruins, presented a room that rivaled a Best Western for comfort, but with far more charm. As different as they were, the two rooms shared one trait: They were there when we needed them. In Foncebadón, I had Sue to thank for not having to sleep with the rowdies in a roomful of bunks in the basement.

At breakfast the next morning, Gert shared that there had almost been a fight the night before in the dorm.

"A guy on a lower bunk was snoring very loud. The man above him yelled louder and louder for him to stop. Finally, he poked the snorer with a trekking pole."

Gert said the snoring man woke up to an angry man peering over the edge of the bunk, holding the pole. The snorer leaped out of bed and tried to pull the guy with the pole off his upper bunk, but the men in the next bunk held him back, narrowly averting a fight. Gert had been shaken by the incident.

Dorm room snoring was a nagging issue, but most pilgrims combatted it with ear plugs rather than trekking poles. For light sleepers, no set of ear plugs silenced the chorus of tired trekkers sawing logs. The resulting lack of sleep was a common complaint. I taped narrow butterfly-shaped strips over the bridge of my nose to maintain silence. They must have worked because I never got poked with a pole.

Leaving Foncebadón, we found ourselves alone on a wide path downhill toward a distant remote valley. Sue and I had walked at least a mile when we sensed that something wasn't right. The guidebook described an uphill trail to one of the most famous landmarks of the Camino. We turned around and unhappily retraced our steps uphill to find the pathway, relieved that we had discovered our error before we had gone farther.

Back on track and after a 20-minute, 300-foot climb, we reached another iconic Camino landmark. It was the Cruz de Ferro, the highest point of the trek at 4,934 feet. I had prepared for the moment months ago at a cemetery in California. There, I gathered three small stones from the graves of Mom, Dad and my nephew Danny, who died when he was just 30.

Cruz de Ferro's iron cross sat atop a wooden pole several stories high. For centuries, pilgrims have placed stones at the base. Traditionally, the stones represented worries that would be left behind. As we arrived at the monument, several giggling young women posed for photographs at the pole while a bicyclist rode up the stone pile and raised his arms in celebration.

I had pictured a more solemn scene. I looked at the three stones cradled in my right palm. Dad's was biggest, and I remembered kicking the hard turf next to his grave to pry it loose. I trembled slightly as I scanned the cross where the celebrants showed no signs of leaving. I had expected that the moment would stir feelings, but I was unprepared for their depth. I enveloped the stones in my hand, stepped up the slope made up of centuries of others' memories, and laid the rocks near the base of the cross. The women and bicyclist continued shooting the breeze and laughing, oblivious to my mission.

I walked down the mound with a dull ache in my chest. As I turned toward the long, steep descent from the Cruz de Ferro, I inhaled deeply, and my legs followed Sue down the trail. However, my heart and attention remained with the stones at the cross. I searched for the mysterious source of my emotion and it appeared quickly. It was the biggest of the stones, Dad's. Why?

Closure was elusive as I found Dad in my mind's photo album from the twelfth year of my life, one of my most difficult times. I sat cross-legged on the linoleum floor in our 50-by-8 trailer, staring at my father. He was seated at the small dining table and pursed his lips stiffly as he studied an open newspaper. He looked much older than 64, but child-like in size.

Questions came to my sixth-grade mind, but I couldn't bring myself to verbalize them.

"What are you thinking about, Dad?"

Dad often appeared to be sad, but I could only wonder why.

"Why did Mom, Joe, and I move away?"

My brain turned to another page, which held a picture of the one-room quonset hut where Mom, Joe, and I slept on a mattress on the floor. I had been aware for years that we were poor, but I realized a new level of poverty every time I came home to the run-down hut. I never learned why we left Dad for part of my sixth-grade year.

I turned to glance again at the Cruz de Ferro.

But twelve-year-old Reg had more unspoken questions.

"How will I learn to be a man, Dad?" The question had surfaced in a big way that year.

Then the one that mattered most.

"Why don't you love me?"

My childhood reflections were as clear as the trees that lined the Camino as I followed Sue down the mountain. I paused to collect myself, but my journey through time continued.

I was 21. Dad, 73, had returned to California several years earlier, a homecoming that disturbed me so much that I couldn't speak to him. His mental and physical health had deteriorated while he was in Canada, and he lived in several care facilities after he returned. By my junior year of college, I had softened and visited him occasionally.

As I continued to follow Sue downhill, I pictured my final nursing home visit. Dad sat in the depressingly gloomy room. He was skin and bones, nearly lifeless. I turned to depart for the hourlong drive back to my apartment near UCSB. I paused to look at my father from the doorway.

"See ya, Dad." His deep-set eyes peered out from the dimness like they saw nothing, then he suddenly gazed at me. His mouth opened, his quivering lips moved.

I heard nothing, but saw the words, words that I would have treasured when I was 12.

"I love you."

But, as a young man, the words didn't resonate. I withheld a response, walked out the door and drove home.

Ten days after I left him at the nursing home, I sat in the funeral home chapel while a man who had never met my father officiated. At just 21, I would live the rest of my life without a father. But I was not overcome with grief. I was numb. Mom was sad, but I sensed relief, mainly because her husband's years of suffering had ended.

Sue stopped and turned around.

"Are you okay, honey?"

Sue's question sounded like it came from another world.

"You have been quiet since the cross. Are you still angry about the people celebrating up there?"

"More disappointed, I suppose. I have been thinking about Dad."

I removed my glasses and wiped my eyes on my shirtsleeve. I was not ready to say more.

We soon passed a spartan albergue in an outpost called Manjarín. The proprietor, Tomas, built a hostel for 35 pilgrims amongst the rubble. The guidebook described an "outside toilet" and water from a well on the other side of the road. The spectacular snow-capped mountain views were tempting, but Tomas' albergue was too rustic for us.

One of the most treacherous sections of the Camino jolted me fully into the present. Rocky, hairpin turns led us nearly 10 miles and 2,800 feet lower. Several young men carried mountain bikes toward the mountaintop as we descended. I doubted that they carried stones to deposit at Cruz de Ferro. When we finally arrived in Molinaseca, we checked into the Hostal el Palacio, next to the Rio Maruelo and a major upgrade from our usual lodging. Hostals are similar to pensións, lodging houses generally cheaper than hotels but pricier than albergues. Our room was €45 with picturesque river and mountain views. It had the most luxurious bathroom of our Camino, featuring sleek, dark tile, modern fixtures, and a glass door on the oversized shower.

Normally, after my backpack slid off my shoulders at the end of the day, my next stop was the shower. On our 18th day of trekking and after 233 miles, my backpack took its place on the floor and I found a viewpoint in a chair next to the open French door and a second-floor Juliet balcony.

I watched pilgrims stream over the nearby arched stone bridge spanning the river. Most were just passing through on their way to Ponferrada, a city of 62,000, three miles away.

My heart was turning a corner.

I was not proud of my meltdown at the end of the previous day in Foncebadón, but I had accepted it as part of my experience. The old Reg would have focused on his regrets for days or longer, like I did in fifth grade when I blurted out words that I would regret more than any I had ever spoken. An obnoxious parrot had deposited the fateful words in my memory bank. During an art project, the girl sitting at the desk in front of me turned around and grabbed my scissors.

"Give them back, you son of a bitch!" That's what I yelled, and the consequences were immediate.

"Go sit outside, Reg," snapped Mr. Schneider, my teacher, pointing to the hallway.

"Son of a bitch!" That's what the parrot had said, over and over, at my family friend's mobile home the weekend before. I had no idea what it meant, but the kids at Rio Real School repeated the words beyond teachers' hearing range untold times, just like the parrot. Everyone laughed—hard—except me. I was mortified, and the scene replayed in my mind for several … years. I have longed to be able to laugh whenever the memory resurfaced, but it has jabbed me almost every time.

There was one more thing. I needed to come to terms with my disappointment and mental detour about Dad at Cruz de Ferro, which I knew would take time.

I was determined not to allow my ruminating to rule the rest of my life. I told myself to let nagging memories pass like the people who walked over the bridge. My dream was to transport a Camino Reg, who would be filled with serenity, back to California with my backpack.

As I sat next to the balcony, bright sunshine illuminated our riverside room. Conversation from the bridge delivered a gentle hum of sounds. A warm breeze brushed against potted flowers on the balcony.

"This is the life," my inner voice celebrated.

21

Was He Wearing Purple Leggings?

As the sun began its daily flight across the Camino, we said goodbye to Molinaseca, which had been a restful pause. The early mornings were times of leisure for bar proprietors in the town, so hopes for an early breakfast faced "*Cerrado*" signs at every window. Our only choice was breakfast in Ponferrada, three miles away.

After just a few steps, Gert emerged from a side street.

"Reg and Sue! Where have you been?"

I pointed to the hostal. "We stayed there last night. How are you, Gert?"

"I am fine. My wife will meet me in Barcelona next week! So, I have many miles to do in a short time so I can finish the Camino." I could see the anticipation on his raised eyebrows.

"That's wonderful, Gert. Best wishes to you!" I said as he accelerated out of town.

It would be the last time we would see Gert on our trek. People come and go on the Camino, but I will know Gert forever.

Midway through our hike to breakfast, two young male voices approached from behind. They were talking too fast for me to understand more than a word or two of their Spanish.

"Buen Camino." I expected them to return my greeting as they passed.

Instead they slowed to our pace and hiked next to us on the wide path. They wanted to get to know a couple of old folks from California. Daniel and Luis, from Barcelona, looked about 18 and switched to English as Daniel asked us where we had started. I quickly noticed that Luis would have to work hard to keep up with Daniel's long strides.

"We started in Pamplona," I answered. "And you?"

Daniel finished a long drink of water. "We began in St. Jean and have been walking almost three weeks." My mental calculations concluded they were probably averaging more than 16 miles a day.

Their backpacks caught my attention.

"You have small packs. You must be having your luggage transported."

Daniel shook his head. "No, this is it. Just one extra set of clothes, a poncho, a light sleeping bag, and a few bathroom things."

Their packs probably weighed less than half as much as mine.

"How did you get so much time off school or work?" Sue asked.

"We took a year off school," Luis said.

He added background. "Our parents did the Camino together over several years. Now it's our turn." The boys looked at each other and nodded.

Daniel and Luis sped ahead after talking with us for several more minutes. They were particularly curious about our sons and their travels.

When I was 18, I doubt I would have considered what Daniel and Luis were doing. And a gap year? It wouldn't have occurred to me; unfortunately, it is not part of American culture. But I envied what they had and were doing at such a young age.

As Sue and I progressed toward Ponferrada in silence, I reminisced about my senior year in high school when I turned 18. My best friend, Craig, was everything I was not: strong, good looking, popular, at ease with girls. Plus, he had a great dad. Craig and I became close quickly after we met during the summer before our last year in high school. I was thrilled that a guy like Craig wanted to be my friend. When I wasn't at my newspaper job, his family's house was my second home.

As the summer drew to a close, I dreaded another year at Oxnard High. One sunny afternoon as we hung out on the beach, Craig had an idea. "Why don't you transfer to Hueneme?"

I had never considered the possibility of going to Craig's school. Hueneme was Oxnard's arch rival, but my Yellowjackets loyalty was thin. I had one extraordinary friend—Rebecca—at school, but she was offset by others who treated me like a punching bag. Plus, I knew I would still see her. Mom loved Craig and was all for the transfer. She even helped me get a doctor to write the required note that said it would be better for my (mental) health. I was ecstatic.

Craig and I may not have walked the Camino together as 18-year-olds, but my 1961 VW Beetle transported us on several camping escapades. We cooked beans while driving to Yosemite National Park by propping cans on the floor next to the blazing-hot heater vent. We smoked too many cigarettes and drank a little Coke with our rum. We laughed so much our sides hurt, like when we freaked out as a raging bear was about to attack us in our tent. It turned out to be a growling raccoon eating our food, which we had left outside. Because of Craig, his friends, and others I met at Hueneme, it turned out to be the best year of my young life.

On May 3, Craig accompanied me in Spain for a while. I heard his laugh and corny sense of humor. I felt the warmth of his friendship. A lump in my throat arrived along with a revelation: Craig had been the first person who had many friends, but still called me his best friend. If only the confidence he brought out in me could have accompanied me to college.

As we neared Ponferrada, I considered Daniel and Luis and wondered how the Camino would have affected me when I was 18. Would albergue dorms and pilgrim meals have given me the nerve to sit at a table of strangers in the college cafeteria? At UCSB, I was the new kid in school again, but it was a university, a foreign place to me and anyone else in my family. I felt so conspicuous that I ate meals in an empty corner of the dining hall. I no longer worried about my clothes or bullies, but I was a stranger in a roomful of kids who had trained for college all their lives. The chair under me barely got warm, as I shoveled my food as fast as possible, then disappeared back to safety. After dinners, I slid into a cubicle on the top floor of the library to try to study. I yearned to jump into my old VW bug and drive away from college for good, but again, I couldn't bring myself to disappoint Mom. Finally, during my second freshman term, I found an off-campus dorm and a small circle of friends along with part-time jobs that anchored me.

Ponferrada, a spectacular city built next to the Rio Sil and Rio Boeza, greeted us with a 12th-century Templar castle that featured a series of turrets and flapping flags. Extensive renovations had returned it to splendor. The Camino snaked alongside impressive historic buildings and across from the castle we found a cozy restaurant, late breakfast, and a familiar face, Clement, the young Irishman. He sat at an outside table with a couple of trekkers also in their twenties; their backpacks leaned against a stone wall next to the castle.

The last time we had talked to Clement, he had descended a steep trail from a detour to view castle ruins during our first week in Spain.

"We are waiting to tour the castle when it opens," Clement told us as he sipped coffee.

"I can't resist the side trips. They make long days, but they are usually worth it." He wore the smile and friendly eyes that I remembered.

I reached for my wallet. "How much for a dose of your energy, Clement?"

"I have slowed down a bit, just 12 or 13 miles a day now."

"So you've come down to our level. If we hadn't gotten a helicopter ride on the meseta, you would be way ahead of us!"

I wanted to give Clement and his fellow trekkers a chance to drink their coffee and digest my lame humor, so I gave a little wave as we continued through Ponferrada.

"Enjoy the castle!" I shouted back.

Clement and his Camino friends had been walking together for several days. Like Clement, many came to Spain alone, but didn't always travel solo for long. The trail offered solitude during the day, except for regular "Buen Camino" greetings from passing pilgrims, but life inside the close quarters of albergues was another matter. They were not the best recharging stations for introverts, or even tired extroverts, but they were fantastic places to make friends.

We ended our 24th day in Spain, and 19th day on the trail in a town whose name would bring snickers from young children (and two mature walkers from California): Cacabelos. We fancied the Cacabelos stamp in our passports, so we decided to spend the night. After showers in our upstairs La Gallega pensión room downtown, we sipped beer while sitting in ubiquitous plastic chairs along a narrow street. We watched locals and trekkers amble by. Sue pointed out we had not seen any familiar faces here, a rare occurrence.

A four-mile climb the next morning brought us to Villafranca del Bierzo, a small village with charm and historical buildings, including another large, impressive stone Templar castle. We faced a decision after crossing the bridge over the Rio Búrbia. We could go straight, the Pradela route, and climb 1,400 feet to Alto Pradela, where the guidebook promised stunning views. Thick, view-obscuring cloud cover made that an easy decision. The other trail paralleled a road in a narrow valley to Trabadelo, just seven or eight miles away. Like a river, we took the path of least resistance.

The footpath paralleled the tree-lined Rio Pereje and a two-lane road. We would get teased later at happy hour for taking the painless way. "What was the point?" I asked. "It was too cloudy to see anything from the top."

Our next decision needed no defense. There were several albergue options in Trabadelo, but as we sauntered through town on the main road, we stopped at a four-room pensión, El Puente Peregrino. The two-story, stone-walled building faced the river and advertised dinner and breakfast menus. We stepped into the small bar that doubled as reception. It had the feel of a pub in a quaint English village. Elly, a pretty Dutch woman with tightly cropped hair, greeted us with her excellent English. Our upstairs room was like an English B&B with a double bed, side tables, and lamps. Next door was a shared bathroom with a tub and something we had not seen in Spain. I couldn't resist, stepped on the scale, and it confirmed my suspicion: I had lost five pounds, even though I had consumed enough calories for two pilgrims. We rinsed clothes and hung them on a clothesline on the small terrace. After muscle-soothing hot baths, we set out to explore town.

As we stepped uphill toward a tiny church, trekkers dragged themselves down from Alto Pradela. They looked wiped, and I tried not to appear too refreshed, but I was thankful it was not me descending the mountain. We returned to the pensión where Elly and her Spaniard partner Santiago joined us for Saturday afternoon beers on a long bench outside the bar. We enjoyed a river view and abundant sunshine. A dartboard that hung from a side door tempted me to challenge Santiago to a game, but I settled for conversation. He was quite the talker and remembered when Martin Sheen and his movie crew came through the area and filmed a segment in nearby O'Cebreiro.

"He walked the wrong way through O'Cebreiro in the movie," said Santiago, who wore a V-shaped growth of facial hair from his lower lip to his chin. I enjoyed his story and had no doubt he would have accepted my darts challenge.

I glanced at Sue. "That will be a good reason to watch the movie again when we get home."

As Santiago added details to his movie story, I noticed a wide-brimmed Crocodile Dundee-style hat and baggy shorts over purple leggings approaching from up the street. The mustachioed man who wore them stood at least six-four. A petite woman was next to him. We had seen the couple along the trail several times, but had not gotten beyond "Hola" and "Buen Camino." They could see we were a fun group, so they stopped next to the bench and asked where we got our tall glasses of beer.

Santiago darted off to fill beer orders while we all introduced ourselves.

"England, Papua New Guinea and New Zealand" was Geoff's answer to Elly's question, "Where are you two from?"

"We moved from England to Papua New Guinea and taught there for most of our careers. We retired to New Zealand."

Papua New Guinea? I had never met anyone from that country. I almost asked if there were really head hunters there.

"Our friends told us we were nuts," Sue said. "The people are quite illiterate, and most do not speak English. In fact, the country has more languages than any other place."

"I thought I was adventurous when I took a job in a one-room school," I said.

As Geoff weaved tales of teaching adventures in Papua New Guinea, I realized where I had seen him before—as a World Wrestling Foundation performer on TV. Not really, but he looked the part, and his personality fit—larger than life. His irreverent sense of humor, partnered with a twinkle in his eyes, was more intoxicating than the Spanish beer in my glass.

Unfortunately, Geoff and Sue left us to return to their albergue for dinner. They missed Santiago's skillful touch in the kitchen. In the rustic pensión bar, Elly served tomato soup, vegetarian lasagna, and chocolate crepes from Santiago's kitchen. All delicious, plus a good red wine, definitely not watered-down like we had been served several times.

The next morning, Santiago served the best coffee of our Camino along with fresh orange juice, bacon, eggs, and fried potatoes. It turned out we would need every ounce of the breakfast fuel for what was ahead: one of the steepest challenges of the Camino.

O'Cebreiro is among the trek's most celebrated villages. Its elevation of 4,297 feet required us to climb about 2,300 feet, transporting backpacks on sore shoulders. Shortly after leaving Trabadelo, we discovered Geoff and Sue sitting on a bench near the trail. We had seen them walk enough to know she was a fast, determined hiker. Her husband seemed strong enough, but followed a different drumbeat.

We couldn't resist a distraction from the impending climb and, more importantly, another chance to spend time with the New Zealanders, so we joined them. Soon, it was story time on the Camino.

Geoff sat like a schoolboy who had misbehaved as Sue described the moment she reached the mountain pass west of Pamplona near the beginning of their walk.

“I turned around when I got to the top, and there was no Geoff! I ran back, looked down the path, and I still didn’t see him. I yelled his name as loudly as I could. I was near panic!”

I shook my head at Geoff. His mischievous smile told me the best was yet to come.

She continued her story. “I looked up at the white windmills way up on the ridge. There was a man waving his arms!”

“Was he wearing purple leggings?” A chuckle from the bad schoolboy gave me my answer. His wife threw me a serious glance.

“It was him!” Sue confirmed with frustration and a long sigh. California Sue and I erupted in laughter, but it was clear Kiwi Sue had not found his stunt amusing.

“You’re bad, Geoff,” I snickered.

“Reg and Sue, let me explain. I saw a trail go off to the left and told myself, ‘No one is going this way. I’ll see where it goes.’” He flashed an innocent face that belied his guilt.

I understood Kiwi Sue’s exasperation, but part of me wished I could be more like her husband. If only I was able to laugh like Geoff when I got into trouble.

I could have listened to their stories all morning, but Sue (my wife) and I heard the call of the mountains. We bid the New Zealanders adieu, for the moment. The six or seven miles to Herreries twisted along the Rio Pereje in a lush, green valley and ended with a gentle rise to the small village. The steep climb we had anticipated was next. We passed a hillside of purple flowers waving in pleasantly warm sunshine before an even steeper slope. We paused to rest two or three times and finally reached the quaint village, a bar, and confusion. We were exhausted and glad the climb was over when we found a bench in the shade near the bar on a narrow, winding, cobblestone street. I bought two tall lemonades in the bar and returned to the bench, where Sue had spread our fresh bread, cheese, and orange slices.

I had taken my first bite when Kiwi Sue came around the bend after her climb. I scooted over to make room, and she welcomed the chance to sit.

She shook her head and sighed. "Geoff took the road. I told him it was longer, but he said it wouldn't be as steep."

As the three of us ate our late lunch, I said I was relieved we had made it to O'Cebreiro.

The New Zealander looked for a sign that I was joking.

"This is not O'Cebreiro."

It was my turn to seek a sign.

"That's funny, Sue. You almost had me there."

Her words extinguished my smile.

"No, I'm serious. This is La Faba."

She showed me the guidebook map and elevation chart. My heart sank as I absorbed the unwelcome reality. It was no Mt. Everest, but three miles and 1,200 feet additional climbing awaited. And there was no Sherpa guide to carry my backpack.

Sue stayed behind to wait for Geoff, who had still not arrived by the time we finished lunch. The trail was mostly shaded, but it was warm — in the 80s. It was the steepest uphill part of the Camino so far with rocks that poked out of deep, quicksand-like mud that threatened to envelop our shoes.

I turned a switchback corner and found myself face-to-face with the ugliest four-legged pilgrims I had ever seen. I leaped off the trail just before two huge bulls passed, nearly at my eye level. We had seen cattle several other times, but never up close. A rancher in a bright blue polo shirt followed, holding an eight-foot long pole. His dog brought up the rear. Loud snorts escaped dripping noses as the cattle stomped by. Thankfully, there were no drips from the other end.

Our mood was soon lifted by three trekkers, two women and a man.

"*Buenos dias!*" All three greeted us cheerfully.

"Race you to the top!" I was not sure what made me say that, but perhaps one reason was, despite their youthfulness, the trio didn't exactly look sporty. I had a chance.

"No old man is going to beat me," the taller of the two women said. I peeked behind me and realized she was talking about me.

Friendly teasing continued as the five of us stepped carefully around the mud and rocks.

"See this pole?" I said as I held up a trekking pole to the woman behind me. "It has a bad habit of tripping anyone who tries to pass."

Sue and I gave it everything we had and gradually surged ahead of the whippersnappers. Actually, none of us set any speed records, but when we finally reached the top, Sue and I were relieved to see that this time it really was O'Cebreiro. And for once, I had kept up with Sue on a climb.

We stood victoriously at the mountaintop, surveying the expansive valley far below. Sweat dripped into my eyes, and my back was soaked, but I was energized. It was one of the highlights of my Camino. I felt like a conqueror, not because I finished ahead of the three "kids." For one day, it was my Mt. Everest.

"Would you like me to take your photograph?"

I turned around and saw the teen-aged boy who had made the offer.

He snapped one of our favorite photos from any trip we have taken. He perfectly captured the exhaustion and exhilaration written simultaneously on our faces.

It was a warm, beautiful Sunday in the mountaintop village, and I was charmed by the festive, family atmosphere that was unlike any we had experienced in other towns. A lively mariachi band delivered a special vibe as the costumed musicians played in a small plaza next to the O'Cebreiro Iglesia, one of the oldest buildings on the trek. Crowds milled in the gift shops next to cobbled, winding streets. Tourists tapped their feet to the music as they sat at outdoor tables and sipped cold drinks. A few pilgrims with backpacks wandered through. I was awed by the spectacular views of the surrounding mountains and valleys.

During three weeks on our journey, we had mostly avoided studying the guidebook entries for villages ahead. We knew a little about some highlights, but skipped over many details. Our strategy had its liabilities, like a couple of hours earlier, when we wrongly assumed La Faba was O'Cebreiro. But the rewards were the surprises around the corners and in the villages. O'Cebreiro was one of the best eye-openers yet.

In search of beds, we moved down a sloping, narrow street to the end of town and the albergue Xunta. There was plenty of room at the modern, 104-bed hostel. It had been renovated, and a bed would cost €5. But, the dorm we inspected had room for at least 40 foul-smelling trekkers, 38 more than we had anticipated.

We turned around and hiked back uphill to a hotel near the church. The Santuario do Cebreiro had one room left, upstairs and just above where the mariachi band played. It was delightfully medieval in character, except for the modern en suite bathroom. It cost €55, expensive for the Camino. As I looked around the room, I was aware that we were getting spoiled.

After a much-needed cleansing, we had drinks in the lively bar downstairs with a couple from Berkeley, California. We had gabbed with them briefly several times along the way. They were about our age and strong walkers. He was a retired school superintendent and remembered our names from a few days before. I was delighted that we were on his memory radar.

Roger asked me why I was wearing wide rubber bands around my right wrist.

"It reminds me to focus on one step at a time. When I get filled with messy thoughts from the past, I pull on the rubber bands and let go. I usually snap out of it."

He smiled. "I could have used those in my job!"

After drinks, Sue and I wandered through gift shops. I was on a mission to replace the rubber bands with a Camino-themed bracelet. Not a style accessory or a good luck charm. I wanted something that would remind me that my mind could be unburdened of my past and my noisy inner critic.

The first store offered bracelets made out of beads, weavings, and plain leather. Nice, but not what I wanted. The next shop, just beyond a lively bar, presented one small rack of bracelets. I scanned several spindles before I found it: black leather, about a quarter inch wide. A round, nickel-colored piece of metal was attached with a scallop shell molded into it. When I fastened the clasp of my bracelet, its message was clear: Focus on the present with a quiet mind and move forward like the lines on the shell.

The scallop shell was my preferred trail marker. Sometimes, it was embedded in stucco walls or in the sidewalk. Its significance was centered on the shell's contours, which merged at the end, just as the many Caminos and people who met in Santiago. Scallop shells dangled from many trekkers' packs.

O'Cebreiro was one of our most memorable experiences in Spain. In three weeks on the trail, we had walked 270 miles. Sue and I had been talking on the trail about what we had learned. With about a week to go, Sue wrote on our blog:

There have been mornings when getting out of bed has been difficult. A restless night, a cold room, tired feet, an aching back, snoring, wind, rain, and for some (fortunately not us), even snow, cause weary pilgrims to think twice about lacing up his or her boots.

However, the promise of each new day keeps us all going forward, toward Santiago ... toward the end. The journey has been filled with so many memories. Had I stopped to take photos of everything that caught my eye, Reg and I would be two weeks behind schedule. As it is, we should arrive in Santiago in about a week. I expect to find more surprises along the way. More memories to be made ... a good reason to get out of bed!

It was 96 miles to Santiago, but I hoped the voyage would continue for the rest of my life.

22

Bolt From the Blue

"Honey, come see this." Sue pointed at her iPad.

"What is it? I'm hungry; let's get breakfast." I expected another comment from a reader of our latest blog post from O'Cebreiro.

"I think you'll want to read this e-mail first."

Mom and Dad,

Bad news. I have to go back to work in Yosemite right away. They need me to open the river raft stand early. Gail can't come with me yet because she has to finish the semester. I don't want to leave her. See you in Mariposa when you get back.

Chris

The bolt from the blue left us exchanging looks.

The younger of our twin sons, Chris had been living in Morgantown, West Virginia for the last year. His note arrived after several years of on-and-off, but mostly off, communication.

"Who's Gail?"

We both asked that question.

"It sounds like we will meet her this summer," Sue said.

Chris' e-mail filled me with hope. Hope that his life had taken a turn. Hope that our relationship was making a comeback.

Over breakfast at a noisy O'Cebreiro bar filled with customers and the smell of coffee, Sue and I contemplated Chris' e-mail.

Sue knew I had worried for a long time about our son. "I told you things would be all right with Chris. Maybe the year in West Virginia was what he needed."

"I can't wait to see him and meet Gail." My son had a big job ahead of him. The raft stand was a lucrative business for the Yosemite concessionaire. I was proud that he had been given the responsibility again to set up for its busy season.

I considered Chris' e-mail while I donned an extra layer and my jacket for a 13-mile, 2,100-foot descent to Triacastela. A cold front had moved into O'Cebreiro during the night, and it left me wishing for a thicker coat. As I marveled at mountaintops peeking through the clouds around us, I envisioned Tom, Martin Sheen's character in *The Way*. The Camino helped Tom find peace with his son, Daniel, as he sprinkled his ashes at favorite places along the path. Tom's struggle reminded me of the strain of my relationship with Chris. Like Daniel, Chris was rebellious. Like Daniel, Chris dropped out of college. Daniel defied his dad and set out to walk across Spain. Chris couch-surfed across the USA, ate gas station hot dogs and slept in closed campgrounds. Like Tom, I had criticized Chris' choices. Like Tom, I had not heard what my son was saying. Like Tom and Daniel, Chris and I were father and son, but sometimes strangers. Unlike Tom, I still had my son. I had never given up hope that we would find a way back to each other.

The Camino is not a wilderness trail. Unlike the Appalachian or Pacific Crest trail, it is not a place to get away from it all. It is often wide enough for a car or even a truck. There are narrow, rocky, difficult sections, but a village or city appears every few miles most of the way.

The downhill path from O'Cebreiro paralleled a road, which was close enough to the passing cars to play state license plate Bingo if we were in the USA. We paused at a hilltop pilgrim sculpture that featured a bearded trekker wearing sandals, holding a staff, and bracing himself against the wind. Sue was snapping a photo of me next to the medieval model, my head at his belt level, when an American voice broke the silence.

"Let me take a picture of you both."

"Do I know you?" I almost asked after I saw her blond hair and bright green backpack.

As she took our photo, I felt like a tourist for one of the few times on the Camino. I almost said, "Cheese!"

"Thank you," Sue said as the woman returned her camera. "Would you like me to take one of you?"

"Yes, please."

After the woman crossed the road to rejoin the path, Sue challenged my memory.

"You know who that was, don't you?"

"Um, not exactly, but she looked familiar."

"That's Brenda. She's the one who told me she couldn't find anyone more interesting to talk to than the sheep. That was after we had walked and talked on the trail for at least half an hour."

"Yeah, I remember. She took our picture in a field. It must have been three weeks ago."

Our destination, Triacastela, was named for three castles that no longer existed. An oak-forested valley followed the Rio Oribio through the town of 900, where we found a modern room in the Complexo Xacbeo albergue. The village couldn't have been more different from O'Cebreiro. Pilgrims seeking peace and quiet would yearn for an extra day in Triacastela.

It was one of few stops since Pamplona where we didn't see anyone we knew. I missed the reunions that had become part of our routine. The cold and damp weather was probably keeping people indoors, but other than Brenda on the trail, I had not even seen a familiar face.

"What happened to Geoff and Sue?" I wondered aloud while we returned to our room after dinner.

"I hope we'll see them again," Sue said. "Who knows. Geoff may have taken another detour."

"I don't envy him. I don't think I could keep pace with Sue."

I could barely stay up with my wife Sue much of the time.

As we ate breakfast in our pensión bar the next morning, I read an alarming bold-faced note in the guidebook:

Santiago city is now only a week away, and pilgrim numbers increase exponentially from this point, and accommodation is often full.

Our next port of call was Sarria. It is best known as the starting point for those who want to earn a compostela by traveling the minimum distance, 100 kilometers, or 62 miles, to Santiago. The guidebook entry left us with questions.

Would we have to book every bed or room the rest of the way? How crowded will it be on the trail? Would some of the people joining the Camino in Sarria be noisy and obnoxious on the trail, like we had been told? So far, the walk had been anything but crowded. There were long stretches where we could not see other trekkers in front or behind us. The solitude gave me a chance to recharge, a benefit of starting in April.

By mid-afternoon, the trail took us across the Rio Sarria to tall, wide concrete stairs ending at Sarria's Rúa Maior and the first of 10 albergues. The city of 13,000 was home to a busy train and bus station for incoming walkers. Backpackers milled about as we hunted for our albergue. Most pilgrims we saw in Sarria lacked the veteran Camino look—their faces were fresh, their packs were clean, and their footwear looked as if it came straight from boxes.

We had reserved a room at Los Blasones, a two-story albergue near the center of town, right on the path. A short-haired woman took time out from cleaning the front windows to greet us.

"I will drive you to your room."

"Can't we walk?" I asked.

"Your room is back at the entrance to town." It took a moment for us to realize that the location would mean trudging a considerable distance (and back up the long stairway) for dinner and again the next morning as we left town.

"Is there a room in this building?"

"Only a dorm. I have a small one that you could have as a private room." She pointed upstairs.

I looked at Sue, who nodded.

“We would prefer to stay here, thank you.” We were both relieved that we could stay in the main part of Sarria.

Our host led us up a narrow flight of stairs to our small bunk room at the end of a dark hallway.

After our host had departed, Sue wrapped her arms around herself and shivered.

“It’s freezing in here!”

We unrolled our liners and sleeping bags on the bunk beds. Our room lacked a heater and the temperature was dropping. We unfolded blankets from each of the four beds and draped them over our sleeping bags. I considered requesting more blankets, but it was not exactly the Hilton, or even Motel 6. There were no towels, but that was normal for the albergue dorm rooms, so we used our small backpacking towels. Lately, I had been spoiled by larger, fluffier towels in private rooms.

I was relieved—momentarily, at least—when I found the shower room down the hall, where I tested the water and found it was as hot as the room was cold. It would feel great to warm up. As I pulled off my shirt, I noticed a window without a curtain. I was wondering if someone might see me showering when my answer appeared through the glass. I almost waved, but turned away as the passing woman glanced at me. The window opened to the indoor stairway. My entire body was in view of anyone coming down the stairs. The frame was bare; no place to hang my shirt or towel to block the view. I know what Old Reg would have done, but, for one quick shower, Camino Reg bared all.

Showered and freezing again, we sought a toasty bar along with the warmth of pilgrim conversation. We would find both and much more. We opened the door to the first bar along the street, and a short, elderly server greeted us enthusiastically and pointed to chairs at the end of a table. The place was as loud as the Tadich Grill in San Francisco, where on several occasions I had enjoyed great drinks, fabulous seafood, and permanent hearing damage. I yelled our drink order, but had to repeat it when the server held his hand to his ear. It was by far the most raucous atmosphere we had experienced.

Speaking of loud, I glanced across the room and saw the Methodist minister we had met two days before. Kevin was traveling alone. He was from the Midwest, and quite the talker—and drinker, as we would learn. He waved enthusiastically, jumped up from his seat and joined us at our table just as our drinks arrived.

"Reg, Sue, good to see you!"

Kevin's voice traveled well enough to grab the attention of everyone at our table.

Their glances were all Kevin needed to introduce himself (and us) to our table mates and soon-to-be Camino friends. We quickly learned that Hugh was yet another pilgrim who was celebrating his 60th birthday by walking the Camino. But, he had a unique approach, and he stretched his voice so we could hear his story.

"Malcolm here (he pointed to the man sitting across the table) joined me today; he is coming with me to Santiago. Three other friends have each done part of the Camino with me. They have returned to England, but will meet us in Santiago with all our wives for my birthday party next week."

We all raised our glasses to toast Hugh's upcoming birthday. I was captivated by Hugh's tag-team tour with his buddies, but before I could learn more, Kevin took the floor.

"Hey, look at the beer I found." He held up a bottle with a blue, white and gold label. "I'm taking it home to use in a sermon." He laughed as we passed the bottle around. The label advertised "Mahou" beer with "sin" printed under the name. *Sin* is a Spanish word for without, and sin beer is low alcohol. Kevin related his outrageous idea for a sermon, and we all laughed hysterically. It was sacrilegious and not like anything I had ever heard in a church.

When I first met Kevin at a rest stop miles earlier, he came across as self-involved, perhaps trying too hard to impress. But, he was growing on me. I wondered how his humor went over with his congregation. I knew one thing: He was not the kind of guy to hold back, and I envisioned sermons by a man who may have been a born stand-up comic.

We found dinner down the street in a refreshingly quiet, Italian restaurant. I could taste the aromas, and my pasta dish with sausage was a treat. So far, I had eaten more pasta on the Camino than during our Italy trip.

Our albergue room greeted us with air so cold that we immediately crawled into our liners and sleeping bags beneath two wool blankets. Wearing several layers plus my jacket, I waited for my shivering to stop when I realized we were above the albergue kitchen. My nose was reminded of the restaurant we had just left. My ears remembered the bar as noisy cooks made sleep difficult. Sarria had lived up to its reputation as a busy meeting place.

The next morning, we ate breakfast in the same bar as the night before, but it was far more peaceful. We faced a new reality: increasing crowds and perhaps the end of the Camino as we knew it. I felt like I was part of a mob of trekkers as we launched into the 14 miles to Portomarín. One group of about 30 prayed, blocking the trail. "Get a church!" I almost said it out loud as I detoured around them, walking through weeds bordering the trail. The crush of travelers had been enlarged by day-packing groups and fast-moving bicyclists. Crowds jammed trailside cafes, with lines of customers waiting to order.

The numbers of trekkers had increased exponentially—the guidebook was right—and I felt like I had been punched in my gut. I knew the Camino was not mine, but the new Camino was not the experience I had come to know either. I hoped that Portomarín would hold the secret to restoring the magic. Over the next 10 miles, we gradually climbed 1,000 feet before the steep drop to the bridge spanning the Belesar Reservoir along the eastern side of the town.

Portomarín's story was intriguing. A village of about 2,000, its original buildings were flooded in the 1960s when the reservoir was formed by damming the Rio Miño. Prior to filling the reservoir, many of the buildings were taken apart, brick by brick, and rebuilt in the new town. One was the rustic Church of San Juan, with its unique castle-like facade. Our room was in the modern Pensión Arenas on the attractive town square. It had been a more difficult than usual hike, so we were eager to shower and find a bar for drinks. We hoped we would reconnect with people we knew.

We were in luck. Sitting outside in the square on the warm late afternoon were 60th-birthday Hugh and Malcolm, sipping beers with a tall Dutch man who had shared trailside conversations with us several times. All wore Teva sandals, like many trekkers did at the end of the day.

I looked around the otherwise near-empty plaza. "Where did the crowds go?"

"I think many were day-packers, so they probably caught buses."

"Right, Hugh. So, Malcolm, how was your first day?"

Before Malcolm could answer, Hugh interrupted sharply. "He almost ended my Camino, the twit! I'd walked hundreds of miles with three other friends. And then, Malcolm—on his first day—tripped me just as we left our albergue. I was lucky I was not badly injured." Hugh scowled at his companion as he finished his story.

It was an awkward moment, and I felt bad for Malcolm, who folded his arms and looked away. I assumed he had not tripped Hugh on purpose. At the bar in Sarria, I had gotten the impression that Hugh was a kind, happy-go-lucky sort of guy.

We were all victims of comedic timing, though, as Hugh broke into a wide grin. He raised his beer glass, put his arm around his friend's shoulders, and shouted, "Cheers!" Laughs and chugs of beer all around. The Dutch man doubled up and almost fell out of his chair. More laughter, storytelling, and another round of beers made it one of our happiest happy hours. I would have loved to watch Hugh and New Zealander Geoff battle for Camino comedian of the year. I would nominate Ian of England to compete as well. Hugh and Malcolm departed early the next day so they could stay on track for their rendezvous with the other three birthday trekkers and all their wives.

I secretly wished Hugh and Malcolm would invite us to join the celebration in Santiago. Unlike so many times in my life, I would have jumped at their invitation. Before I met Sue, I sometimes wondered if I would end up a lonely old man like Dad. As a single adult, I played on my newspaper's slo-pitch softball team, but almost always said, "No, thanks" after games—for years—when invited to join my teammates for pizza. As I sat home alone, eating my Kentucky Fried Chicken post-game meals, I was painfully aware that I was missing a good time with a great group of people who could become closer friends if I had allowed it. What had I been afraid of? Was I protecting myself from losing friends, which had happened over and over when Dad uprooted me? One revelation from this journey had become clear, and it sounded so simple: Nurture friendships with commitment and trust.

Before looking for a place for dinner, I noticed a couple sitting on a rock wall on the plaza. We had seen them on the trail a couple of times recently, and we approached them to say hello. Dave and Swee Lin had started in St. Jean.

Sporting a gray beard, in the style of Abe Lincoln, his long strides kept him well ahead of Swee Lin. Barely five feet tall, she followed slowly behind and often appeared deep in thought.

"Dave, what are all those papers you are holding?"

"Our bookings. I reserved every night before leaving Canada."

I was impressed. He was the first we had met who had booked the trip himself. Most traveled day-by-day, and those who wanted to book the entire trek usually used tour companies. We had a pleasant pre-dinner visit and, like often happened, our bond would blossom over the coming days. Our Camino family was expanding again.

After dinner, as I walked through the bar in our pensión, I was jolted by a voice from a large group.

"Reg!"

It was Kevin, the Methodist minister from the Midwest.

He introduced me around. I declined a drink offer and realized it would take several to catch up with Kevin and his friends. After chatting for a while, I rejoined Sue upstairs. I would not see Kevin again. Perhaps he got up early and beat us out of the gate. Kevin was another Camino friend who grew on me as time passed. Was he on a research mission for future sermons in his church? He sure could spin a yarn, but I detected plenty of depth.

23

The Solution Was Simple

I awoke so anxious about the crowds that I persuaded Sue to leave Portomarín after an unusually early coffee and toast. We climbed through a thick forest to a road we would crisscross several times during the day. I missed the quiet, more rural Camino. A thundering commotion behind us drowned out the sounds of passing cars. I spun around, gazed wide-eyed down the hill, and immediately shouted to Sue.

"Honey, run for your life!"

The bulls from Pamplona had run across Spain and were about to crush us in their stampede. Their nostrils were flared; their brows were furrowed. We felt the pounding of approaching hooves. Loud snorts echoed. My heart pounded.

Okay, they weren't really bulls. But there were at least 50 trekkers trudging up the hill behind us. And, I swear, their nostrils and brows mimicked those of stampeding bulls.

We sped ahead for the next several miles and arrived at a cafe in Gonzar before most of the crowd, ready for our second coffee.

"Ah, that's better," I said to Sue as we sat at an outdoor table. I sipped my Americano and took a bite of a croissant. But, within several minutes, the place became as crowded as a sidewalk cafe in central Paris on a sunny Saturday. I approached the counter to get a napkin and was elbowed out of the way and slammed with a backpack—by accident, I think. Soon, several day-packers stood next to our table, eyeing our empty cups and plates.

"Are you leaving?" one asked.

I shot them an annoyed look, stood up, and said, "Let's go, honey."

The late-comers lacked respect (or at least it seemed so) for the pilgrimage and for those of us who had been here for a month. I was the one with the furrowed brow until I glanced at the scallop shell on my bracelet, which represented merging paths, people, and their ways of life. I may have felt like my home was invaded, but it was not my territory. I had been too quick to judge. Time for an attitude adjustment, but it was going to require more than a glance at a scallop shell.

We had to do something. The solution was simple, and it just might work.

The gentle climb continued and we stopped for a picnic lunch outside a cafe. As we talked about where to stay that night, we knew we should avoid Palas de Rei, the end of the stage. Lots of beds were available there, which would likely lead to another stampede the next morning.

Sue pointed to Eirexe in the guidebook.

"How about this place?"

It housed two accommodations: an albergue with just 20 beds and a small pensión. No big cities anywhere nearby, so there would be no morning rush-hour traffic. We would be out of sync with the masses. A phone call in my improving Spanish netted us an en suite room at Mesón Eirexe for €35.

Eirexe turned out to be a village that made a postage stamp look big. A canopy of large shade trees covered our path to the stucco-sided, white pensión, where a woman greeted us in Spanish. My mom would have called her "pleasantly plump," as she described herself and my little brother before puberty turned him into another Spittle beanpole. The room felt like a bedroom in an old Spanish home, with religious paintings on the walls. A window brought a shaded back yard lawn into view. As we unpacked, the woman returned, holding something worth its weight in gold to Sue.

"*Señora, tengo algo para usted,*" (Madam, I have something for you.)

She held out a hair dryer. Sue was thrilled with her treasure of the day. A charming host, a comfy room, a sleepy village, and a hair dryer to boot.

Sue enjoyed a steamy shower while I lay on the bed. I awoke to the sound of the coveted hair dryer coming from the bathroom, but I closed my eyes again and visualized Spain's splendor. I had hiked 321 miles, a distance my feet would have dismissed as unfathomable a year before. I was just 45 miles from Santiago, where I would stand before the cathedral like millions of others had done over centuries. My adventure was nearing the end.

I realized my emotions in the past few days had little to do with the crowds and their behavior. I had begun the trek further outside my normal experience than I'd ever been, but the journey had blanketed me in a kind of tranquility I had never thought possible. The Camino de Santiago was the most secure place I had ever lived, despite the fact that my location changed nearly every day. I was moving, like I had so many times as a child, but the Camino was a trail of acceptance. There had been reminders of my past, but rather than retreating into my shell as I had done most of my life, I now basked in comfort, knowing I had nothing to prove. The trail was a quiet recharging station and the bars, albergues, and dinner tables were gathering places of shared respect.

I inhaled deeply, closed my eyes and told myself once again: "My Camino must not end in Santiago."

Sue and I ambled across the quiet, shaded village road to the only bar/restaurant in Eirexe. It was housed in a nondescript ranch-style stucco building. We started with drinks while we sat at the bar.

"Where are you from?" asked the barrel-chested bartender as he poured our glasses of lager from the tap.

"California." In Europe, we got a more positive response if we said, "California" rather than "the USA."

"You are the second couple from California today. The other people lived in Berkeley."

I wondered if he was referring to the retired school superintendent and his wife we had last seen in O'Cebreiro.

"You must have customers from all over the world." I was fishing for specifics.

"Yes, of course. Let's see … today, people from South Korea, Germany, England, France … where else? Um, Brazil and Portugal. Many Spaniards too."

He wiped the bar next to us after removing two dirty beer glasses.

I had read that Spaniards made up nearly half of pilgrims on the Camino. A few days before, I had been thinking of Americans who mount USA maps on their recreational vehicles and fill in the states they visit. It gave me a Camino idea: I could attach a world map to my backpack where I could mark the nations representing people I had met. So far, I would have filled in Brazil, Mexico, Australia, New Zealand, South Korea, China, Croatia, France, Germany, Italy, Spain, Denmark, the Netherlands, England, Scotland, Ireland, Portugal, Poland, Canada, and the USA. There were others I had forgotten and many people whose nationalities were left unknown. The river of humanity that flows across northern Spain represents more countries than any place on the planet except for the United Nations, or maybe the international terminal at London's Heathrow.

I liked the bartender. "Your English is great. What other languages do you speak?"

"Thank you. Spanish, of course, and a little French and German. Most people who come in here speak English."

I took another sip of the Spanish lager, which tasted superior to the beer in eastern Spain, where our journey began. The food was improving too, especially in Galicia. Another idea came when I finished my drink. Were my taste buds connected to my heart, which had fallen head over heals for Spain?

On our way to our dinner table, we stopped for conversation in "Frenglish" with two older French women we had befriended along the trail. We saw them again at breakfast the next morning after a quiet, restful night. None of us was fluent in the others' language, but the French women knew far more English than we knew French. Our conversations were confusing at times, but all four of us enjoyed trying. Questioning looks brought rephrasing and finally nods, most of the time. Or just chuckles.

Our mid-stage strategy had worked. The bulls from Pamplona must have found lodging beyond Eirexe, so during our 13-mile jaunt to Melide (another mid-stage stop), our moods brightened under cloudy skies. We followed the N-547 highway, which intersected the path nine times within 16 miles. It wasn't as annoying as snoring roommates, but road noise filled most of the day's sound waves. Beautiful woodland sections enhanced an otherwise tedious trail that edged roads and passed light industrial areas.

A reunion enlivened our day. Out of the blue, Canadians Stan and Sylvia caught up with us as we rested at the top of a hill. The fact that they were still walking together told me their marriage still had a chance. Their cheerful moods also indicated that they wouldn't need to appear on the Dr. Phil show with their kids and grandkids in a last-ditch effort to save their marriage.

I waved and shouted "Buen Camino" into the Go Pro camera attached to Stan's chest.

"Why did you do that, Reg? The video is running. Ah, well, I can edit you out." He laughed.

"Like you can edit out all the arguments you have had with Sylvia, eh?" That brought a laugh from his wife. Another good sign, I figured.

We stopped for lunch under a rickety shelter as the rain became heavy.

Over hot coffee and deli sandwiches, we exchanged a few Camino tales, and Sylvia shared that their daughter had called several times.

"She's hoping we move in together again when we get back to Canada. It is so important to her that we have family gatherings at the house again."

"No pressure there, eh?" I said.

"But they know Stan and I want it as much as the rest of the family."

"A question, if you don't mind."

"Sure, Reg," Sylvia invited.

"Are you happy that you chose the Camino for this experiment?"

Stan and Sylvia glanced at each other for a moment and nodded before he reached over and held her hand. I wondered if I should have asked the question. It was clearly an emotional moment for them. After lunch, the speedy Canadians raced ahead. Unfortunately, we would not see them again. They were unforgettable members of our fluid Camino family.

As my legs moved in a moderate walking rhythm in light drizzle, my attention leaped ahead to Stan and Sylvia. The Camino (so far) had worked its charm on their marriage. Would it work for others? There are many niche Camino tours. Religious, school, food, bicycling, and more. Why not a tour to mend damaged marriages?

I entertained myself as I imagined the advertising.

"Rip up your divorce papers and leave your troubles at home. Travel the path to reconciliation by walking the Camino de Santiago in romantic Spain. Conquer the hardships and challenges together as you follow in the footsteps of millions."

I smiled as I considered an alternative.

"Rediscover romance while sharing dorm rooms with sweaty, snoring pilgrims."

Or:

"Share romantic dinners with hordes of famished, slurping trekkers seated in metal or plastic chairs at long, narrow tables."

Seriously, I admired the Canadians' commitment. It took courage at a time many couples would just enter a courtroom with their lawyers. No backpacks needed.

Sue and I have rarely been on different pages about the important things in life, although the trek had its tests. There was the time I wanted to walk with fast-moving Ian of Oxfordshire. I even suggested that Sue ride the bus with Ian's wife Marion when they were both fighting foot problems. I backed off quickly after Sue's reaction and wondered how I could have been so stupid to verbalize my selfish idea. Also, Sue would have stayed in coed dorms almost every night, not necessarily to sleep near smelly trekkers, but to save money. She compromised.

For me, the Camino had illuminated many aspects of my marriage. Nothing had compared to raising three children, but the journey had bestowed incomparable riches on our life together. It had strengthened our resolve to stretch ourselves through challenges far outside traditional travel itineraries. But as we neared Santiago, my experience left no doubt that my love for Sue had deepened, if that was possible.

I squinted at the patches of blue sky. I had been so lost in introspection that I hadn't noticed when the rain stopped, but my jacket sleeves were dry, and my hat brim no longer dripped.

The Camino crossed more rivers than I could count, but on our current stage there were eight. Most of the bridges have been around for centuries, supported by stone archways. Many spanned small creeks, but some transported trekkers safely over wide rivers.

In a well-known scene from *The Way*, Tom leaned on a bridge's stone siding and loosened his backpack that contained his son's ashes. He watched in horror as the pack flipped over backwards into the wide, rushing river. Panicking, he ran to the end of the bridge, around to the river's edge and jumped in. He battled the current and retrieved the pack. When the scene was filmed, Martin Sheen, then 69, performed the act himself after a stuntman said it was too risky. Sheen wanted Tom to show how much his son's remains meant to him. For Sheen, a devout Catholic, the movie was about people loving each other.

I failed to recognize the bridge where Tom's pack fell into the river, but the scene came to mind many times as I walked over fast-moving rivers. I stayed away from the edge every time. I would never jump in a river, even to retrieve my backpack, especially when there were no stuntmen around to fish me out.

Late in the day, in a swampy area, we hopped from stone to stone as an army of toads loudly sounded the alarm. Or, they may have been laughing at my awkward use of trekking poles to keep my shoes dry.

Our last stop of the day was Melide, a city of 8,000 in the middle of a guidebook stage. Melide was not as faceless as cities in California that are dominated by strip malls, but the city's storefronts and cafes lacked the character that we had seen in Spain. Cars were parked bumper to bumper along the main street. While looking for a place to stay, we considered the Albergue Xunta until we saw it had 156 beds in seven dormitories. It was modern and cost just €5, but was too big for us. We opted for an en suite room at the Chiquitín for €30. The pensión was at the far end of town, buried among a confusing tangle of side streets.

I took advantage of the strong Wi-Fi to plan the final days of our time in Spain. I booked an attic room in a small hotel a mile or so from the cathedral in Santiago, beginning Monday night. It was not an ideal location or room, but little else was available. I reserved three nights and booked our Thursday train trip to Madrid for our flight back to California. The train had just five seats left.

When we entered Pamplona 31 days ago, our arrival in Santiago seemed ridiculously far away, in miles and time. I anticipated collecting my compostela at the Pilgrim Office in Santiago. I wondered if I would witness the swinging of the giant incense burner, the *Botafumeiro*, a ritual often performed—but not every day—during the mass in the cathedral. There were other uncertainties. How would I feel when my journey ended? Would I be reunited with members of my Camino family in Santiago?

K. 50,0

24

Hand Over That Plate!

For the thirty-second time since we set foot in Spain, I splashed soothing hot water on my face to complete my morning shave. I brushed my teeth and tucked my toiletries bag into a narrow crevice in my tired red backpack. My body rebelled at the idea of carrying it yet another day. Sue sat in a chair and finished her taping-of-the-feet ritual.

It was 8 a.m., and we had just returned from breakfast in the dining room downstairs.

The walking time had struck.

"If we were home, we would be sipping our second cup of coffee while we read the news on our iPads," I said. "And we would still be an hour or two from breakfast."

Sue nodded. "I used to think that was the life. Now I can hardly wait to see where my shoes will take me."

Sunlight filled the room as I pulled the curtain aside.

"No rain gear this morning, honey."

It had been wet on recent days, and Sue preferred to err on the side of caution rather than stop on the trail and hastily don waterproof clothing in the rain.

As we left Melide, I spotted a three-foot-tall concrete signpost that halted me in my tracks. It was engraved in red letters below a blue square that enveloped a yellow scallop shell. The sign read "50." Fifty kilometers to Santiago. Thirty-one miles. I remembered another sign, one we saw in eastern Spain. It announced "725 km to

Santiago." The number had overwhelmed me, and I had wondered if we would really be able to hike that far. Now I wanted the end-of-the-Camino reminders to stop. I turned away from the 50-kilometer sign without feeling the impending joy I had expected would fill me at the marker. Sure, there were times when my backpack felt like a ball and chain, but it was a vital part of my liberation.

It was Saturday, and our shoes would carry us to Arzúa, another mid-stage stop, just eight miles away, our shortest day. Lush green growth lined the wide gravel path, shaded by tall, leafy trees. The Camino occasionally emerged from the forest, revealing rolling hills and farmland. After two hours of peaceful meandering between noisy crossings of the highway, a bar and two familiar faces stopped us again.

They sat at an outdoor table in the brilliant sunshine and waved. It was Dave and Swee Lin, the Canadian couple with whom we had shared several enjoyable meetings. I was particularly fond of the quiet-spoken twosome.

"May we join you?"

"Sure," Dave said. "You should get some coffee. It's good here."

I returned with a cup of coffee and much more. The bar offered something I couldn't resist: eggs over medium with a mountain of fries (or chips). Swee Lin exhibited her infectious smile when she saw my second breakfast, but I was immediately distracted by a booming male voice behind me.

"Sorry, bloke, but hand over that plate!"

I turned around to see a tall, gray-haired Englishman looming behind my chair, arms folded, eyeing my plate. Eyes from neighboring tables turned my way.

"Get your own!" I bellowed.

Our audience laughed.

The Englishman patted me on the back and returned to his table, where four amused fellow trekkers watched.

At the beginning, we had tired of the nightly pile of fries that came with pilgrim meals, but that morning I could have eaten two plates full. I dipped them in egg yolk and ketchup, then stuffed several into my mouth at once. I looked up in time to see that my gluttony had not gone unnoticed. I was able to contain my grin enough to chew with my mouth closed. Finally, I could speak again. I searched for a way to deflect everyone's attention.

"So, Dave, have your reservations worked for you?"

"Yes, every single one."

I figured Dave and Swee Lin must have had more confidence in their trekking and injury avoidance abilities than Sue and I did. Weather, injury, and unanticipated rest days would have sabotaged any set schedule for us. Dave was among a minority of trekkers who wore running shoes instead of hiking boots or shoes. I was surprised when he said he didn't have any problems with them. I wondered how his shoes performed in the rain and mud.

I wished we had met Dave and Swee Lin earlier. Our chance meetings with familiar faces were a coveted part of our passage. It made me wonder why I didn't live in the moment years ago. I used to race through the days at my elementary school teaching jobs, convincing myself I was too busy to take a few minutes to exchange a few words with colleagues. At 49, I began teaching at the college level. I had more time, and I surprisingly took more time. Colleagues would drop by my office for a chat. Close friendships followed and work became more enjoyable. The Camino confirmed another life lesson: "Take time."

"Hope to see you along the way," I shouted to Dave and Swee Lin as they departed while we waited to use the bathroom. They waved, and I noticed that Swee Lin was again many steps behind her husband. I wondered if they hiked apart to bask in the solitude, perhaps even trying a common practice that I had employed: walking meditation. I sometimes counted "one-two" repeatedly in time with my steps and soon found myself lost in an almost hypnotic state. The sights, sounds, and smells along the trail enhanced the experience. The stories that got me nowhere stayed behind.

The warm, bright sun accompanied us as we came to a picturesque medieval bridge over the tree-lined Rio Iso. We were just minutes from our destination of Arzúa, and it was too early to check into our accommodation, so we had good excuses for another bar stop. We sipped cold lemonade at a round table outside under an umbrella at the riverbank bar.

Three robust-looking pilgrims—two women and a man—barely in their twenties, took off their packs and leaned them against chairs at a sunny table next to ours. We exchanged "holas" before they rushed to the bar.

"Two days to Santiago, honey," Sue announced.

I was thinking of words from the past. "You were right, you know."

"What do you mean?"

"Remember what you said last year when I kept saying we couldn't walk the Camino?"

"But what if we can?"

"That's it. I don't want to jinx it, but I think we're going to make it."

Sue took a sip of lemonade before responding. "Physically, I'm tired, and I am looking forward to sleeping in my bed."

I imagined Sue saying, "Ah, my own bed," as she slipped under the covers when we got home.

I gazed at my backpack leaning against a chair. "I am ready to ditch the backpack and the shoes, but I am not prepared for the end."

I finished my lemonade and watched the young trekkers return to their table with tall, cold glasses of beer. The backs of their shirts were drenched in sweat from their backpacks. They clinked glasses with each other and took long swigs.

"I wish I could feel like this for the rest of my life." I said what I had been thinking for days, even weeks. "It is as close to 'no worries' that I have ever been."

"You *can* feel like this forever. It is up to you."

Sue was right.

"Plus, this is just the beginning of trekking for us. I want to do more."

Sue verbalized what we both had known.

We had walked about a quarter mile after our break when I was stopped by Sue's question.

"Where's your hat?"

My expensive, waterproof, wide-brimmed (and nerdy) hat was not on my head.

"Ah, crap. I must have left it at the bar."

My pack stayed with Sue as I quickly retraced my steps down a steep hill to the bar.

"Is that your hat?" The young male trekker at the table next to ours pointed to a chair at the table where we were sitting.

I plopped my hat back on my head, thanked him, and hurried back toward Sue. When I reached the hill, something happened that I had only experienced in dreams. I flew up the hill, with my shoes barely touching the path. Without my backpack to anchor me, it was exhilarating. My legs were still thin, but they were infinitely stronger. I felt like I was flying.

We checked into our room at Rúa on the way into Arzúa, a city of 7,000 known for its cheese making. In the common room, I printed our Santiago-to-Madrid train tickets. After hearing tales of woe from others who did not book travel to Madrid, I was glad I listened to my type-A inner voice. For some, a 12-hour local bus was the only alternative.

Our walk around town left us longing for familiar faces and a friendly pilgrim meal. We turned along a narrow, winding alley, where we caught a whiff of fine Italian cooking. Mama, working in a tiny kitchen at the back of the restaurant, took orders via servers' shouts. We feasted on red wine and fresh pasta with enough garlic to allow us to experience its aroma through the next morning.

We awoke Sunday on a crisp Mother's Day. On the path from Arzúa we passed a burly farmer in his forties preparing for spring planting, guiding a plow behind a large horse that huffed and puffed. The rows were straight, the chunky, dark earth rich. I smelled the moist soil. It felt like springtime. Wearing jeans and a vest jacket, the farmer was one of the youngest we had seen. His farm bordered the wide path that also traveled through woods and cattle ranches. I found it impossible to ignore the too-frequent signs counting down the distance to our destination.

Twelve miles took us to our first end-of-stage stop in several days and a gift that couldn't have been more fitting. We were the first to arrive at O Burgo, the smallest of several albergues and on the uphill road leading into town. A large, private en suite room was ours for €35. As I showered, I struggled to stay in the moment and tried to ignore the fact that O Pedrouzo was our last stop before Santiago.

While Sue cleaned up, I found the common room at the front of the building. I looked out the large window at the street-side courtyard surrounded by a six-foot stone wall. What was that? It was a hat, moving left to right on the sidewalk on the other side of the wall. I caught glimpses of an ear and the top of a backpack with each step. The hat was big, and the man under it had to be more than six feet tall. Was it really him? It had to be, but I wouldn't know for sure until I saw his legs.

I ran out the front door, through the wooden gate and shouted after the man in the purple leggings, who walked next to his wife. "Geoff! Sue!"

They halted and whipped around wide-eyed.

"Reg! We haven't seen you for ages." Sue said as she threw her arms into the air.

"Is there room in this albergue?" Geoff asked.

"The dorm room is nice and is empty right now." New Zealanders Geoff and Sue had always stayed in dorms as far as I knew. He was ready for a beer, so we made plans to meet up after they checked into the O Burgo and got settled.

I hustled back to our room to tell Sue the good news.

"Guess who's staying here!"

Sue had a quick response. "Geoff and Sue."

My jaw dropped in disappointment. "How did you know?"

"By how excited you are."

She was right. I was happy to spend my last night on the trail with the adventurous New Zealanders. The four of us had drinks and dinner in an informal restaurant filled with Spanish families. After Santiago, Geoff and Sue were also going to Madrid for a few days before flying to England to visit family and friends. I asked them what they planned to do in Madrid, and his answer caused his wife to frown.

"I have to see a bull fight!" he announced. It was obvious he would be going alone.

I was hoping for another hysterical story from their Camino, but Geoff and Sue, like us, were distracted by Monday's finale and conversation was comparatively muted.

For the first time in weeks, sleep was elusive despite the comfortable, quiet room. The Old Reg and the Camino Reg were debating how to answer a question.

What would arriving in Santiago mean to me?

25

Why Are You Limping?

The Santiago de Compostela Cathedral soared impressively, and its bells tolled a welcome as we marched into the city. A beautifully landscaped tree-lined path guided us to the larger-than-life symbol of Catholicism. The rhythm of our strides brought peace as we neared the end of our walk across Spain. Pilgrims with backpacks surrounded us. Some limped; tears flowed. Anticipation blossomed with each step; we were a family coming home at last.

I had no idea when I had finally found sleep, but when I awoke, my dream had left behind colorful images of our final day on the Camino. The time that had seemed unreachable for so long was upon us, concluding 29 days and 366 miles afoot. I smiled as I replayed our Irish host's shouts on our first full day in Spain: "Welcome to Pamplona … you are officially pilgrims!"

Reality rudely rained on my dream and romantic expectations. Most trekkers on our final day, a Monday, set out early in order to attend the noon mass at the cathedral, so we were the only backpackers in sight when we departed our albergue. We planned to attend the mass on Tuesday, so we had enjoyed a leisurely breakfast. We walked through swaying eucalyptus trees, and several miles later the trail bordered a tall metal fence around the end of a runway at Lavacolla international airport. The sound of jet blasts replaced the church bells I had imagined.

We snacked and drank coffee near a monument honoring a visit by Pope John Paul II and descended on blacktop and concrete through not-so-attractive suburbs to the busy streets of Santiago. No cathedral stood tall for our view until later in the day. Cars zoomed by, and fast pedestrians brushed past us during a sun-baked stroll that seemed interminable.

We had hiked several miles on hot pavement when the first sharp pain shot up my right leg. It repeated itself with each step and soon my left leg hurt too.

"Why are you limping?"

"It's my shins, probably because of the pavement."

I untied my poles from my backpack. I had put them away for the first time on the trek.

"Maybe these will help."

"You must have shin splints."

My trekking poles took an edge off the pain.

My senses were under attack. Towering highway signs replaced the humble yellow arrows. Sounds of revving engines and honking horns filled the air. Puffs of cigarette smoke wafted from two middle-aged pedestrians in front of me. Pain shot up my shins with each step. My head throbbed. We stopped several times to get our bearings so we would not get lost. At one confusing intersection, a passerby tapped me on the arm and pointed to the sidewalk in front of me. "Gracias," I said with relief when I saw the imbedded scallop shell. The symbol guided us the rest of the way.

The Camino, however, would not allow me to end my journey in that frame of mind. When the cathedral came into view, we neared the north facade, where three musicians played a light-hearted tune as they bounced side to side. A busload of tourists and a sudden influx of backpackers (Did they also take buses?) joined us as we walked through an arched, covered entryway and down another set of wide stone stairs. This time, I welcomed the crowd. Their energy electrified the atmosphere as we entered Obradoiro Plaza, the size of several soccer fields. I turned to my left and immediately recognized the skyscraper-height, dark Baroque towers of the west facade of the Santiago cathedral.

Sue and I embraced and posed in front of the cathedral for the iconic "We did it!" photograph. I studied the west entry to the cathedral, where some still approach the figure of St. James on their knees, as the sobbing Joost did in *The Way*. My emotions were more subdued, but I could not hold back tears while I surveyed the plaza. Sue and I removed our backpacks, and the air cooled my sweaty back. I searched for familiar faces while, all around us, phones and cameras snapped celebratory photos. I scanned the foreboding spires, symbols of the great trek we had just finished.

"Look behind you," I said after my gaze returned to plaza level.

Sue turned around as a jogging trekker, still wearing his backpack, kicked his feet sideways as he zigzagged in front of the cathedral. In the distance, a gray-haired couple, eyes closed, knelt next to each other in the plaza, hands pressed together in front of their chests. Their bulging backpacks lay beside them. Two teary-eyed middle-aged women embraced. A few moments later, a group of young pilgrims stood in a circle and threw their hats and caps into the air, cheering like a bunch of high school kids at graduation. If it were Disneyland, there would be a photo booth where trekkers could buy their treasured memory snapped incognito during the celebrations. Just $20 for an 8-by-10 in a cardboard frame.

We crossed in front of the west facade toward the neighboring business district. Just beyond the south facade, I noticed the Pilgrim's Office sign.

"What do you think?" I asked Sue.

"Why not?"

Inside, we stood in a line that stretched up two sets of stairs to receive our compostelas, the coveted certificates of completion. An hour later, I presented my passports to a solemn-looking man seated behind a tall counter. He took just a few seconds to unfold my passports and scan my 62 stamps.

"Why did you walk the Camino?" he asked in a monotone, not even glancing up. I expected more, not just a cursory scan at the passports I had carried for five weeks.

I wanted to shout at him. "Look at them, will you? See all the stamps? Check them!"

Instead, I replied, "Partly for spiritual and partly for personal reasons."

He wrote my name on the Latin-language certificate, and I thanked him as he handed it to me. His eyes traveled past me to the people in line. I rolled up my compostela and inserted it into the thick cardboard cylinder that I bought at the entrance to the upstairs Pilgrim Office. I expected to be asked to explain my answer in order to earn the authentic Latin compostela. I was prepared to say the Camino had moved my spirit deeply in a secular way. He did not check my stamps, nor did he look at the dates. I appreciated the fact that the office was busy and staffed by volunteers, but his lack of attention and enthusiasm disappointed me.

As I walked down the stairs past waiting pilgrims, I realized the Old Reg had gotten the best of me. But that was about to change in a big way. We may have finished the Camino, but its rewarding path was not complete.

Several long streets comprise the core business area of old Santiago. They are connected by narrow alleyways that snake between three- and four-story stone and stucco-sided buildings. It is one of Spain's busiest tourist centers as well as the destination for thousands of pilgrims each month. Bars, restaurants, hotels, and shops fill the street level. Flower baskets hang from upstairs windows and balconies while chairs and tables invite al fresco drinking and eating.

Thirst guided our exploration when suddenly a short woman ran out of a bar, yelled "Sue!" and hugged my wife before I figured out who it was. Then she turned toward me, and I saw Huan, our young friend from Toronto. We had not seen her for several weeks, since the night before Sue's trip to the hospital. I had just gotten my hug when a young Irish male voice emerged from the same bar. More hugs, from Clement.

"Come in, join us! Linda and Quincy are inside, and there is plenty of sangria," Huan invited. We crowded around a table and exchanged favorite Camino stories while we laughed and finished two carafes. I felt like a long lost, loved, family member. Clement, who had shared our first table in Uterga five weeks before, sat across from me. We were separated by at least one generation, but we had just completed an experience that bridged the years. I expected we would each remember the sangria celebration forever.

Later, we finally found our room in a funky building across from a noisy carnival. As we sat propped in bed inside our tiny attic room, Sue wrote a blog post for the final day:

This morning was different. As we tied our shoes and struggled into our backpacks, we knew this would be our last day of walking. Reaching Santiago was always the goal ... until we started the Camino. After our first night in an albergue, we realized that this journey would be about so much more than simply reaching Santiago.

We've each had our struggles; everything from blisters to coed bathrooms. The Camino tests everyone and spares no one. But at the end of each day there is a bed (usually warm), a meal, friendly conversation and laughter. And an eagerness to get up and do it all again the next morning.

We walked into Santiago this afternoon with a mixture of joy and sadness. We had done it! But now what? That is the question we pilgrims are asking each other as we prepare to go our separate ways.

26

All Eyes on the Altar

A thousand of us sat in pews in the Santiago de Compostela Cathedral and waited like pilgrims before us had done for hundreds of years. We gazed at the Romanesque barrel-vaulted ceilings above that contrasted sharply with the pointed features of the Baroque exterior.

Sue tapped me on the arm and pointed at the immense, glittering altar.

"See the incense burner?"

My heart leaped at the sight.

Was it a sign that the *Botafumeiro* would soar high above us in the most anticipated and historic act of the Pilgrim Mass?

I leaned to my other side, to another Sue, and her husband Geoff.

"See it?" I asked.

Sue of New Zealand looked at me with raised eyebrows and nodded.

"I think it is going to happen, Reg!"

Our morning had started with feelings of emptiness. Other than to breakfast and the noon mass, there was nowhere to walk. There would be no trekking destination the next day, either. We had accomplished Sue's challenge, "What if we can?" Instead of relief, we faced another question: "What now?"

A half hour before the noon mass, we filed into the cathedral and stepped along the central nave, past massive columns, side aisles, and signs that showed the languages offered inside the confessionals. In one booth, a priest, eyes closed, awaited a sinner.

We sat next to Geoff and Sue a few rows from the altar in one of two facing aisles perpendicular to the nave. How perfect it had been to find the New Zealanders sitting in a pew next to a pair of empty places. They were the best seats because if the giant incense burner swung, it would pass directly overhead. In just 10 minutes, the noon mass would begin. It was Tuesday, May 14. The audience focused on the altar expectantly.

Other than my short stint as an altar boy in an Episcopal church in Ojai, California, it was the most excitement I had felt in a place of God. While I waited, I closed my eyes to let the peace settle, but instead my brain clicked into memory mode. It was my personal Camino movie, rewinding to Pamplona, April 10, and fast forwarding through my journey across Spain. The high definition picture was wired to my heart. I couldn't resist the pause button.

There I am, a nervous pilgrim at my first albergue in Uterga. First shower, first bunk, first pilgrim meal, first Camino friends. James and Gitta. Ian and Marion. Clement.

Pause there! I see Brazilian Isabelle, laughing at me and holding her drink, bragging that her beer cost less than mine.

What are the bright flashing lights? Ah, the police, the fake taxi, the hospital. Marco the taxi driver to our rescue. I see the doctor's good news for Sue (and me).

What was that? Rewind. I see Frenchman Paul and Gert from Germany, laughing hysterically during the Sorry, Charlie game.

There's another familiar face, the elderly Spaniard who kissed Sue.

Judy! Come back. Sing that birthday song again, please.

I feel freezing air on my back. It must be Castrillo, our challenging detour with Gert. One of the best times ever.

Fast forward. It's my meltdown in Foncebadón.

There we are, outrunning the bulls just after Sarria.

I see countless images of bars, beds, meals. Miles and miles of Spanish scenery. A Camino family that grew and grew. Umpteen memories.

I opened my eyes as several priests and a nun gathered at the altar, signaling the beginning of the Pilgrim Mass. I glanced at Sue (my wife, that is) and took her hand in mine. A priest read the home countries of walkers who arrived the day before. A nun read and sang. Lines formed for communion followed by an interlude.

All eyes were on the altar. Eight red-robed *tiraboleiros* approached as the *Botafumeiro,* nearly five feet tall, was lowered on its thick rope. I gripped Sue's hand; our dream was becoming reality. The pipe organ's booming, bass notes sounded as a green-robed priest lit the coal and incense inside the burner. The music sent shivers up my spine as I imagined what the ceremony meant to those who filled our pew for hundreds of years before me.

Smoke quickly escaped through the holes in the metal as a *tiraboleiro* pulled the burner to one side and pushed hard to propel it across the altar. He joined the other seven red-robed attendants, each holding a line tied to the main rope that traveled over a pulley high above, down to the now-swinging burner. I listened to the nun's echoing song and heard an angel. Two thousand eyes intensely tracked the *Botafumeiro* as the pipe organ and the nun's divine voice filled the cathedral.

The *tiraboleiros* pulled down on the rope with all their might. The incense burner leaped and swung farther over the packed pews. Fragrant smoke swirled, like it had since medieval times, when it helped dull pilgrims' body odor. My neck strained to follow each swing as the burner soared more than 60 feet in the air. A fly had a choice of 1,000 open mouths in which to fly. The nun continued to sing; the *tiraboleiros* pulled each time the burner swung across the altar. I couldn't understand the Latin song, but it didn't matter.

Several people around me wiped away tears. Signs everywhere banned photography during the service, but in acts that struck me as sacrilegious, many held cameras and cell phones aloft to record the drama. I imagined they would be lined up at the confessionals afterward to seek forgiveness.

The incense burner finished swinging above the altar and posed before the statue of St. James.

After the service, Sue and I ate pizza nearby and returned to the cathedral to explore further. Inside, we climbed steps to the side of the altar and soon stood behind St. James' statue.

"He has a pretty good view of the nave," I said as Sue observed from his other side. I felt like I was being rude by standing close enough to whisper in his ear. Tradition held that travelers who reached the spot would thank St. James for the strength that allowed them to complete their journey. Pilgrims were supposed to hug him and kiss his cape, but neither seemed right to me.

We descended steps to the crypt, said to be St. James' final resting place. The pilgrimage had been underway for close to 400 years when, according to legend, Saint James' tomb was found. St. James, one of the twelve apostles of Jesus, had been beheaded in 44 AD in Jerusalem and it is believed that his remains were brought to Galicia.

Our final Camino climb was next: our highly anticipated cathedral rooftop tour. My shins screamed all the way up the stairs, but it was worth every painful step.

"This roof is incredible," Sue said, standing on one of the overlapping granite slabs, each several inches thick.

I gingerly stepped on slabs above the altar. "I am amazed they let people come up here." The angle and height were not for the faint-hearted and I surprised myself that my fear of heights had not appeared. It is one of the tallest cathedrals in Europe at 246 feet. We sat on the peak for a few minutes to enjoy the stunning views of Santiago's rooftops afforded by the clear skies.

We returned to the cathedral the next day in a steady rain for a second Pilgrim Mass and, luckily, another chance to watch the *Botafumeiro* soar. More good fortune came after the service as we shopped for souvenirs. We were briefly reunited with the three Australian engineers at a bar that advertised beer for just €1. Leave it to them to find the place with the cheapest lager. Minutes later, we spied 60th-birthday Hugh from England, his trekking friends and their wives, outside another downtown bar. As we passed, we shared thumbs-up signals as I shouted "Happy Birthday" to Hugh from a distance. At each reunion, the warmth of fond memories filled my heart.

On our final day in Santiago, we sought a taxi ride to the train station. It was the first time we had worn our backpacks in three days, and the weight added pain to my shins. I longed for the train seat and the relief it would provide.

"Look!" Sue pointed at a stream of walkers approaching us in downtown Santiago.

"Vicki, Tom!" Sue greeted the young Texan and her younger brother, who each lugged a large backpack.

"We are going to Finisterre," Vicki shared. Finisterre is known as the End of the World, and for some, it is the end of the Camino. It was another two or three days, and few trekkers take the extra steps.

I congratulated them for going the extra miles. After a few minutes of sharing some Camino highlights, they turned and were on their way.

I realized I had forgotten something.

"Buen Camino!" I shouted after them. Tom pivoted and waved with both hands. It would be the last time I would say those words in Spain.

Sue and I relaxed in the roomy, modern train cabin at the Santiago station as passengers boarded. I stretched my toes and legs and soaked up the comfort. Our 372-mile train trip would almost match the 366 miles we had walked. We would arrive in Madrid in six hours, which roughly equaled our average daily time afoot on 29 trekking days. I glanced across the aisle. Our dog-tired red backpacks rested in the rack above. Inside were battered pilgrim passports with stamps from albergues, pensións, and bars. A cardboard tube held our compostelas.

What else was I taking home?

I ticked off a list of lessons. Privacy is overrated. Never assume. Trust people. I am not a sissy. Take time. Never give up. Stay flexible. Pack light. Be patient. Use poles properly (thank you, Gitta).

An important one: Don't take myself so seriously. Have faith in the Camino's magic.

Another came to me: Cultivate friendships.

"*Todos a bordo*!" (All aboard!) The conductor's words from the platform penetrated the cabin.

I contemplated the lessons. For me, the Camino was a safe zone half a world away from my home. I had not forgotten the towel's snap, followed by the boys' taunts and stares so many years ago as I undressed in the junior high locker room. But I no longer felt the darkness that came with the memory.

There was really just one lesson.

Acceptance.

I must accept who I am and what I have done. I must live with the actions of others.

My fellow pilgrims and I practiced acceptance daily. We persevered through struggles. We appreciated each other and celebrated common bonds as well as differences. We accepted the past, lived in the moment and moved forward.

The train, its movement almost imperceptible, pulled away from Santiago de Compostela, beginning the first leg of my homeward journey.

My walk across Spain had ended, but a new dawn cast light on my path to contentment.

27

My Most Painful Discovery

I gently tucked my empty red backpack into a closet of my Mariposa, California home. It proved its worth on its maiden journey, enduring my sweaty back, hot sun, rain, and innumerable tosses to the ground. It waited against walls outside countless Spanish bars. It was stuffed into crowded jet overhead compartments, taxi trunks, and bus undercarriages. It passed through the hands of a Spanish police officer, a hospital security guard, and airport inspectors.

Crammed full of my clothes, rain gear, toiletries, first aid kit, and food, my pack hugged my back for 366 miles. It carried what I needed without complaint, but it endured nearly constant criticism from my shoulders. It never protested when I jolted it off the ground by one harness. Another thing about my red backpack: It would not remain empty or without adventure for long.

The finality of the physical Camino struck me when I closed the closet door. The trek was neither Mount Everest nor the Pacific Crest Trail, but it presented Sue and me with unexpected challenges. Our achievements were our bonding agents, to each other and to everyone who traveled the Camino de Santiago.

We were happy to be home, but were hopelessly homesick. We missed our Camino family, the daily sense of accomplishment, even the aches and inconveniences.

For untold mornings after our return home, we drank coffee, read the news, and looked at each other with "What now?" We were ready to put on our backpacks and walk to the next unknown destination.

We came back to wonderful friends in Mariposa, but it would take time before they stopped feeling like strangers. Our lives had been transformed in ways we could not explain. Each time I was asked, "How was it?" I couldn't find the right words.

My adventure in Spain was many things to me, but it was no quick fix for my lifelong struggle with anxiety. I am better at staying in the present, and my childhood memories do not haunt me as often as they did before. Why? The Camino stretched me so far that I learned what is really important. The simple things, like a bed, a meal, health, friends and family mattered most (not in that order). I learned that, throughout my life, I had fussed over things that weren't important.

But my mindset is not that rational. I wish Dr. Gaudiani could fix my brain's wiring as well as he fixed the wires in my heart. My consciousness still travels the well-worn paths to worry, just not as often as it did pre-Camino. And it snaps out of dark places faster. The Camino Reg is alive and well, but the Old Reg plots occasional coups.

"But what if we can?"

Sue's words have become my life's theme. At 66, I can't get enough adventure. A year after the Camino, Sue and I backpacked 150 miles on the West Highland and Great Glen Ways in Scotland. In the summer of 2015, we met all our kids in Park City, Utah, for what some family members called the "Spittle Family Frolic." I wish we could have such a family adventure every year.

In 2016, Sue and I walked the Tour du Mont Blanc, 68,000 feet of elevation change over 110 miles in the French, Italian, and Swiss Alps. It brought us to new heights of the Earth's beauty. In 2017, we bought a small travel trailer and drove backroads across America, nearly 10,000 miles, without an itinerary. Sue wanted to title our RV blog postings "Hookups Across America." After some horrified pleas from the kids, we settled on "Backroads Across America."

In spring 2018, we completed another pilgrimage, the Way of St. Francis in Italy. It guided us 256 miles from eastern Tuscany to The Vatican, with nearly 80,000 feet of elevation change. It was a tough hike and we saw fewer than 40 fellow trekkers over nearly a month on the trail. We loved the rugged beauty of the Umbrian mountains.

Each trek has been unique, but they all hold similarities. Surprises appear around every corner and over every mountain. The routine is comforting beyond measure, and each trail has felt like home. Looking back, the treks feel like old friends. I could say I miss them, but they are with me every day.

Carrying a backpack is sometimes a pain, but living out of it is empowering. The world, as big as it seems, is actually small, and my favorite way to see it is by foot. And the Camino Reg dominates my psyche on the trail far more than at home.

Our sense of adventure has taken us beyond travel. In 2014, we moved to Ashland, Oregon, leaving 25 years of friendships and a comfortable life. I worried about settling into a new home and wondered if we would find new friends. Our move to Ashland proved once again that the best things in life are sometimes the hardest to do.

I am still hopelessly in love with the Camino. Distance trekking is a trendy pursuit these days, and the Camino is king, even in southern Oregon. My enthusiasm for long walks led me to teach three trekking courses at Southern Oregon University through the Osher program for 50-plussers. I offered a trekking presentation at the Ashland Public Library in spring 2017; 80 people crowded into the room. I am often asked which of the treks is my favorite. I pause each time to collect myself. It almost feels like I am explaining how much I love my wife or each of my children. Of our treks, the Camino is the most special in many ways. It was our first and longest trek; plus, many of the people we met are still friends. Like other loves of mine, the Camino's allure is in the intangibles.

The Camino trails draw thousands more trekkers each year, causing more people to call ahead to reserve accommodation. I suspect the live-in-the-moment qualities that I found are still present, but trekkers might have to work harder to find them. The plentiful facilities still make the Camino stand out compared to our other treks.

Travel is hard. It transports me to situations that challenge me to improvise and grow. Long-distance trekking is both easier and more difficult than traditional travel. It is more physically demanding in most cases and requires me to adapt to many different types of accommodation, weather, and food. The pathways through countries have unique cultures that wrap their arms around me. On the Camino, Sue and I talked about how the experience could change the world if more people, particularly world leaders, followed the footsteps to a common goal.

Our friend Ian from England shared his perspective:

The whole route was a wonderful experience. We met so many people from so many countries.

I would not wish the world onto the locals, but the world might be a better place if everyone could have the experience.

And there is my most painful discovery.

After returning from Spain, I wondered why the stone from my father's gravesite that I placed at Cruz de Ferro still tugged at me. But it was several years later, while working on this book, that the significance of the written words struck me like a lightening bolt. I wrote about my visit to the mountaintop monument and how it brought me to think about the last time I saw Dad. It was during my visit to his nursing home just days before he died. I was 21 years old. He sat on his bed in his dimly lit room, staring blankly at the wall. I looked at him from the doorway and said, "See ya, Dad."

He gazed up at me and mouthed the words he had found impossible to say to me when I was a child: "I love you."

As I wrote about the scene, I remembered how I reacted to Dad's plea: I withheld a response, walked out the door and drove home. As I typed the words 45 years later, the pain of regret hit fast and hard.

Why didn't I go to him? Why didn't I put my arms around him? Why didn't I tell him what I really felt all along?

Instead, I had ignored his plea. Until now. I vow to forever keep forgiveness and these words in my heart: “I love you too, Dad.”

There is one more aspect of my journey that I didn’t understand until I wrote these pages. I mean no disrespect to Ponce de León, but the Camino de Santiago is my fountain of youth. I drink from the fountain each time I write about my trek. I experience it when I close my eyes and view memories from my steps. Every long-distance trek transports me back to my 366 miles of youth in Spain. But it is a different youth than I lived decades ago. This time, with occasional exceptions, my shadows don’t darken my path.

Afterward: Our Camino family

Remembering my Spanish adventure, I am most nostalgic when I consider the people we met. I am grateful for the Spaniards who made me feel like their home was my home. So many fellow trekkers stand out for their kindness, inspiration, stories, and even their jokes.

The following pages contain updates about members of our Camino family with whom we have been able to stay in touch and photographs from the times we shared.

Sue and I climbed to O'Cebreiro during one of the more exhausting and exhilarating days on the Camino. A Spanish teen-ager took one of our favorite photos from our trek.

James and Gitta are still living in Denmark and have trekked in Italy since the Camino. After our West Highland Way hike in Scotland, we spent a wonderful week with them in Copenhagen and at their beach area homes in North Zealand.

We visited Ian and Marion at their Oxfordshire, England home after our West Highland Way trek. In April 2014, they returned to Spain and finished their steps to Santiago. As Ian reported, "no problems, no blisters, no shin splints, no buses, no trains, no taxis." They are often drawn to France in their motorhome.

Gert has returned to the Camino de Santiago from Germany every year since 2013, except one year when he walked the Camino Portuguese. Sue snapped this photo of me with our friend after he prescribed a cure for Sue's blisters: "More red wine, Sue!"

Our reunion with Clement, the Irishman, was a highlight of our time in Santiago. We exchanged e-mails after we returned home, then lost touch for several years. Just before publication, I checked e-mail one morning, and his name appeared in our in box. He wrote, "It's absolutely wonderful to hear from you. Your e-mail has brought back memories of the great Camino." His note made our day.

Geoff and Sue are still traveling the world from their home in New Zealand. In 2017, they walked the Portuguese Camino to Santiago. Sue reported there were crowded albergues, but the path was quiet. “We are having a great time.” And from Geoff: “The purple leggings are still in use!”

Verna, on the right, is still living in Texas. She and Judy returned to Spain in 2014 and completed their Camino. Verna conquered the West Highland Way and is planning more treks, possibly the Tour du Mont Blanc and the Way of St. Francis in Italy.

Judy, who lives in Australia, has continued her travels, walking the West Highland Way in Scotland with another friend. She and her husband are adventurous travelers through many parts of the world. Her song is one of the best birthday memories of my life.

Canadians Dave and Swee Lin continue to travel the world a month at a time, three or four times a year. They still do treks and have branched out to bicycle touring in Europe. Dave wants everyone to know they still travel light and never check baggage, even when they go for a month. This photo was from the scene when an Englishman (standing behind me, not pictured) had jokingly threatened to take my second breakfast.

Acknowledgments

This book has been a long, exhilarating, and deeply satisfying expedition. But I have not traveled it alone.

My wife Sue contributed in ways that I cannot fully measure with words. It began with her statement after we watched *The Way*: "We should do it." And her repeated response when I doubted if we could walk 500 miles: "But what if we can?"

Her resolve continued as I wrote this book when she sent me back to my MacBook Air laptop with her sometimes blunt critiques. Her willingness to read draft after draft never wavered. Her memories about Camino events, conversations and people jogged mine.

Her artistic gifts brought watercolor scenes, which grace this book's pages. The cover is her design, as is the title.

George Mahood, an English author, supplied the push I needed to begin writing. I wrote to him after I read his book, "Not Tonight, Josephine," which I loved. I told him Sue and I traveled a lot and hosted a blog. He checked it out and wrote back:

"You should think about turning them into books … My trips have always just been for fun too, and then became books later." I have read all his books; my favorite is "Free Country" and if you are a bicyclist (or not), you must read it. George's encouraging words and adventurous spirit inspire me.

Ashland, Oregon author Peter Gibb played an important role. He encouraged me to write, gave me pointers, and read my first draft. His response was supportive, but clear. My draft was not going to cut it, unless I was writing for fun. It was tough to hear, but he was right.

Finally, the Camino de Santiago. It challenged me, cared for me, and led me to places I never imagined possible. I will travel the Camino forever.

I hope you will review my book on Amazon and I would love to hear from you. Write me at

spittlereg@gmail.com

If you want to join my email list for future announcements, please let me know via e-mail.

In Memory

Ron

Santiago: We made it!

Made in the USA
Lexington, KY
06 May 2019